# How your Hand Knitting

# Brenda Hunt

# How to sell your Hand Knitting

## Brenda Hunt

*Marketing for Small Business Series*

*To my wonderful husband for all his support*

# Introduction

Everyone loves the comfort of a beautiful hand knitted jumper or scarf, the cosiness of a beautiful soft throw or chunky cushions or the quirky beauty of a unique bag or soft toy.

You only need to see how many shops, stalls, departments stores and websites sell all the various different varieties of hand knitted designs across the whole spectrum of types and styles of work at the moment to decide that this is true.

And even though it goes through cycles of fashion, knitting is not exactly new.

People have loved and valued hand knitting throughout history, whether it was a lovingly created Afghan, a detailed and protective fishermans sweater, a beautiful, finely worked baby's shawl or a fashionable scarf or bag. Today, hand knitting is everywhere, in every style and at every price range and available to all.

Making your own hand knitted designs takes this love of beautiful things a step further. You can create exactly what you want, choosing your colours, your style and the size that suits you, rather than having to choose from the selection offered to you. It opens up a whole new world of self-expression, you can wear your art as well as filling your home with it.

And now you have taken the decision that you are ready to offer your beautiful handmade creations to the rest of the world.

There are a number of ways of presenting your hand knitting to the public and this book is aimed at helping you to sell it face to face, directly to your customers rather than through shops or craft outlets or online.

What will make your hand knitting stand out from the crowd?

There are some crafts - such as jewellery making or papercraft - that will mean you are competing with a great number of other crafters head on, but knitting craft does separate you from a lot of other crafters at shows. It is a more specialist skill, you have to spend more time on producing your stock and you have a very wide range of products that you can focus your attention on.

You might decide to create unique Christening Stoles, your own range of fashionable jumpers, a collection of home decor, which in itself can cover a huge range from practical carrier bag holders to luxurious bed throws and afgans. You might create funky handbags, practical hats, dolls clothes, soft toys or beautiful cushions. You might produce hand knitting in luxurious yarns or a range of special designs on a knitting machine. The field of knitting is huge and the choice of product to produce is as wide as your imagination.

So whatever competition you find yourself selling against, however large or small it is, this book will show you how to stand out from the crowd, how to succeed not only in-spite of the competition - but because of it!

When you market your hand knitting properly, the fact that you might be surrounded by others who haven't thought about how to display their designs will make your work stand out, it will automatically attract attention and make your designs look even better.

So, this book will guide you through the whole process.

How to create your style.

How to promote your business.

How to layout your shopfront.

How to decide on packaging and presentation.

It will also give you some ideas about where you can set up your shopfront.

Craft fairs are the obvious first step, but depending on what your product range is, you might choose to do wedding fairs, markets, country fairs, or party plan. You might even decide to do all of them!

Whether your aim is to simply pay for your hand knitting addiction, make some extra money for holidays or take the plunge and start your own business empire, this book will help you plan and design and make the most of your exciting new venture.

# What is Marketing and Why is it important?

### Why should you care about marketing?

Why am I starting with marketing? It's because marketing is at the heart of any successful professional venture. In fact, this whole book is really about marketing and how you can use marketing to create your new business and to grow to whichever level of business you want.

Some people will be happy to keep their hand knitting business small, a home business that is focused on one person. Some will expand it to a family business selling on-line and through some craft shops as well as face to face, and others will want to create a brand that will be found in a small number of high end home decor boutiques or fashion stores across the country.

But in this book we are focusing on the early stages of your new business and how to make the best of your opportunities when selling direct to your customer face-to-face.

## What is marketing?

Many small businesses make the mistake of thinking that the whole concept of marketing is only something for big business.

That it's the world of the Marketing Director, huge budgets, huge departments, specialist agencies and the multi-national companies.

But at its heart, marketing is basic common sense.

Know what your customer wants - and supply it.

In fact, it's such basic common sense that some huge multi-national companies, with their huge marketing budgets and high powered marketing departments, completely lose sight of it, and then they lose sight of their customers as they leave in droves and go somewhere else that does still supply what they want.

Think of the mess some of the big high street names get themselves into when they decided that they know better than their customers. They start losing their customers - which for any company, means losing your business - and it can take them years and a huge amount of work to get them back.

Another misconception is that Sales and Marketing are the same thing - but they're not.

A Sales Campaign - selling your idea to the public and persuading them that they can't live without your product, can be a very expensive process. TV adverts, billboards, newspaper & magazine advertising are well out of reach for a small business. The world of the Internet and social media has opened it up if you are savvy with the technology, but it still doesn't get you the huge coverage and it still isn't the same as marketing. Companies can and have, spent huge amounts of money on trying to sell a product but failed at the end of the day because they're failed on the basic principle of marketing - they're trying to sell something that people don't want!

So, although some things may be out of the reach of the small business, really good marketing is something that the smallest of start up business can - indeed have to be - really good at.

After all, if you can't afford an expensive TV advertising campaign you'd better make sure that you're supplying exactly what your customer is looking for!

### Market research

Every successful business knows who their target audience is. Look around at shops, magazines, fashion companies, car companies, holiday companies and of course design companies.

Take one area of business and really look at them in detail rather than just at the ones that you normally buy from.

For instance spend a day at your nearest large shopping centre and study the stores that sell clothes - you need to visit a large shopping centre so that you have a full range of outlets to study.

You may never have really thought about it, but you'll know which ones attract you personally and which ones you'd never think of shopping in. But what is it about the brands and their shops that give you these signals?

This time really look at all of them, really study them.

Who do they target?

What age range?

What style?

What budget?

Decide what type of people would shop in that store.

What age, what life style, what career?

Where would they go for the evening? What type of holiday would they take? What type of car would they buy? And how can you tell that?

For this process, don't worry about being judgmental - you are trying to judge, you're learning how to judge what type of customer is going to want your hand knitting!

Apart from the prices - which might not always be obvious straight away (in-fact the presence or absence of obvious prices can tell you something as well) - how can you tell the difference between the budget shop and the expensive?

What is the difference in the shopping experience between the designer boutique and the outlet that sells quality classic pieces?

Look at the decor of the shops, the colours, the style of their furnishings, the way they use the space.

How do they display their stock? Is every inch of space used or do they display a smaller number of pieces, giving each individual outfit space to be seen? Do they sell a jacket or do they sell the whole outfit as a 'look'.

How do they package their product? You don't actually have to purchase anything, although that can be fun and is certainly a way of finding out how they treat their customers, how they make you feel about your purchase and the whole experience of dealing with the company.

But if you decide that the process of market research doesn't stretch to a £350 Mulberry purse (sad but true!) just find a coffee shop or seat close to the shop and watch customers come and go. Is their purchase just stuffed into a plastic bag or is it carefully wrapped in tissue paper and gently placed in a beautiful, branded bag with ribbon handles? Think of what you would prefer as a customer.

Times are tough at the moment and it seems that they are going to stay that way for a while yet, so parting with money should be a pleasure. The experience should be fun, enjoyable and memorable for the right reasons. After all, when you buy new clothes, chocolates, cosmetics or a piece of hand knitting, it's a treat, no matter how much or little you're parting with, so it should feel like you're getting a treat rather than feeling the same as when you're just buying a tin of beans.

You can see the same range of experiences in almost any market.

A lipstick can be picked up in the supermarket with the weekly shop or it can be a luxurious treat in a beautiful gold case, picked out for you by someone elegant who takes the time to find the right shade for you and then packs it in a lovely gift bag with some free samples of other items in the range.

You might say that a lipstick is a lipstick, but in times of austerity sales of luxury lipsticks go up. Women might not be able to afford the Dior outfit or the Chanel handbag, but they can afford the lipstick or the eye shadow.

## Market research, part two

Now that you've looked at how people shop and more importantly, how companies sell to them, you need to bring your market research closer to home.

Why you're still in the shopping centre, focus your attention on departments and stores that specialise in your area, whether that is home decor, fashion, classic clothing, accessories or children's clothing. You should look at specialist stores, departments in the larger stores and the stalls and barrows that you can also find in the larger shopping malls.

Can you tell what their target audience is? How do they create an image?

Remember, they are the professionals at this and they have spent a great deal of time and money to create the look that they want, the look that will attract the target audience that they want and then get them to part with their money. Learn from their experience!

Although you won't be creating a complete

store or department of your designs, there will still be signals that you can take away with you and learn from.

What sort of colours have they used in their displays? Is it displayed on stands as individual pieces, or are they just piled together on plinths and counters? Is the display crowded like an Aladdin's cave of colourful fibres or does each individual piece of hand knitting have its own space, even its own display stand?

How do they package the designs? How do they physically price it? Is it a price sticker on the tag, does a general price cover every piece on the display or are they priced individually, with special designer tags that tell you what yarms have been used in the piece – alpaca, silk, mohair or cotton?

What signals tell you the price range without even looking at the price?

Once you've actually looked at how things are sold and started to recognise what the subtle signals are in the selling process, you can begin to decide what signals you want to give to your potential customers and how you will go about that.

### Craft shops and events

If you're interested in creating your own handcrafted creations, you've almost certainly been visiting craft fairs, craft shops and gift shops for many years, but you probably haven't looked critically at them.

You now want to start visiting them and looking

with a more detailed eye. After all, you are about to become part of this world. Although you're looking at the overall image you are specifically looking at how they sell both hand knitting and items that may not be knitted but still fall into the same bracket as your work, whether you are competing with leather handbags or linen jackets.

What does the work look like, what image does it create? Without looking at the prices, what price range would you judge that it falls into and who is it aimed at?

What signals make you think that?

When you did look at the prices, are they in the range that you expected or are they cheaper or more expensive than you thought they would be? What is giving you these signals?

Is the work that's displayed giving you the image of pocket money pieces, but is actually priced as exclusive design? Or are you looking at beautiful pieces of hand knitting that you think will be in a higher price range, actually being sold at mass market or even supermarket prices?

Either of these extremes will actually lose you potential customers.

I vividly remember visiting an art market in Florida over 20 years ago. There were many crafters with permanent stalls selling a wide range of items from T shirts and handwoven shawls to novelty number plates and shell ornaments, and I visited it a number of times during the holiday.

One of the stallholders was selling beautiful handmade silver jewellery, beautifully laid out and none of it priced. The designs were very unusual, the display was very clean and uncluttered and whereas many of the other stalls were frequently crowded with potential customers, this one was not. During many visits, I looked at the jewellery and admired it, but I didn't actually go into the store area, because it looked as if it was above my price bracket. Towards the end of the holiday, I decided I had to at least have a closer look at it, I never have been able to resist jewellery! To my absolute amazement it was actually very reasonably priced, costing far less than many of the other tourist items and gifts that were being sold in the rest of the art market. Luckily, I hadn't bought all of the presents I wanted to bring home. So I was able to purchase some of these unique works of art for friends as well as myself. The problem is, if I had only made one visit to this art market, I wouldn't have purchased anything at all from this wonderful jewellery store, because the signals it was giving off were totally wrong.

So when you visit craft fairs, or when you're selling at craft fairs, take a look around at other stalls and see how they display their designs and what signals they are giving the potential customer.

Now that you've learned how to really look, you will be able to pick up on the displays that work and the ones that don't.

Which ones are attracting people and which ones do people pass by without looking. It isn't always to do with the quality of the work. Some people selling beautifully made handcraft items are just not attracting people's attention.

You can continue to learn and fine tune your own shopfront as you do more events. You will learn over time what did work, and even more importantly, what didn't work.

Once you start fine tuning the process, you will discover that different venues require you to adapt your display. A part of the stall that you use to catch people's attention may have to be at the left end of the table in some venues and at the right end in others, depending on which way the traffic moves around the room. I have been known to re-organise an entire 12 foot display halfway through a fair!

### Who is your customer

Now that you have done some serious market research, you can begin to decide who your designs are aimed at.

No matter how tempting it might seem, you cannot be all things to all people, you have to choose who your target audience is.

Where do you want to place yourself, in what can be a very crowded market?

You have to take a number of things into account.

Where will you be selling?

Who will your customer be?

Do you want to sell fashion designs or designer fine hand knitting?

What style of work do you make or want to

make - boho or twinset and pearls? Soft toys or soft furnishing? Trendy bags or classic baby clothes?

You can either decide where you are going to sell and what type of customer you will have and what they will want, and set yourself up to design for that market.

Or you can decide what type of hand knitting you make or want to make and find an outlet that will attract the type of customer for your style and price range.

The problem is that it's not always easy - or possible - to find exactly the outlet you want - either in the area that you are based or at the rent that you can afford to pay - especially at first.

There's not much point deciding that you want to sell high end designer hand knitted jumpers in the finest yarns at upwards of £250 a piece if you can't find a place to sell it from, or Gothic chic in a quiet area that doesn't get a regular supply of Goths to adore your masterpieces.

The beauty about running a small business is that you can be adaptable. In fact that's one of your greatest strengths. You don't have to go through planning meetings, committees, getting approval and deciding on budgets, arranging purchasing, suppliers and mountains of other planning. You can get an idea, decide what you need to do and go and do it! See a trend and be selling it within weeks, sometimes within days. You can constantly adapt and change to a changing market.

So, probably the best way of deciding on your

style is a mixture of what you like making and what price range you think will sell.

Don't be scared to be different. You don't simply want to churn out what everybody else is selling, or copy what you think is a popular style in the local supermarket. Put some of your own character into your hand knitting, that is what will help you create your own distinct style. Whether that is the type of colours that you use, the fact that you make items only using natural fibres, or that you like to include crochet detail in your designs.

Whoever your customer is, one of the real delights of buying a hand knitted piece directly from the designer is the fact that you are buying something that you can't get in the local shops, and that you won't see everybody else wearing.

# Where will you sell?

This book is mainly aimed at the process of selling face-to-face, directly to your customer.

Of course there are other ways of selling your handmade designs nowadays. People often think of selling online first, through etsy, eBay, Amazon or your own website. Or you could decide to sell through craft and gift shops or wholesale to other outlets. And that's fine, but there's still plenty of chances to sell directly to your customers.

Craft fairs
School or church fairs
County shows
Ideal home style shows
Christmas markets
Wedding fairs.
House parties
Markets
Talks to WI or other groups
Demonstrations

You may decide to use some or all of these methods to sell your hand knitting direct to the customer, but if you're looking at this list for the first time, how do the different events differ?

Although you can often make bookings at quite short notice, especially for smaller events that might be planned close to the date or if there have been cancellations at some of the more established events, many booking are made about a year in advance.

You should be prepared to start planning your annual calendar in January to make sure that you are at the most successful events.

### Craft fairs.

This is probably the section you will think of first when you decide to sell your handmade hand knitting direct to the customer face-to-face.

You've probably visited quite a number of craft fairs over the years, but once you step onto the other side of the counter there is actually quite a lot to know about craft fairs.

There's a huge variety in the type of event, the size of event, how much rent you will have to pay, how many days you will have to commit and what is expected from you as a craftsperson.

At one end of the scale, you will find small local events, where you can simply book a six-foot table and pay about £20-£30 for the day. Tables are normally supplied, although for some fairs you do have to supply your own, in which case a wallpaper pasting table is normally first choice but you'll probably move on to a more sturdy version after you've completed a few fairs.

As a general guide, most of these fairs start at

about 10am and close at about 4pm with the venue being open from about 8am to 5pm to allow you time to set up and then clear away again afterwards.

The organisers for most of these smaller events will expect you to be on time, stay to the end of the fair, pay your table rent and sell only your own hand made goods. Many of them will also require you to have public and product liability insurance, although of course you should have this anyway.

Many of these organisers run fairs throughout the year, either a regular event at a specific venue or a programme of events at different venues that repeat throughout the year. As you book more fairs you will get to know more crafts people and they tend to be very generous with their knowledge and will let you know who else to contact about different events.

Customers are often very loyal to a series of events and they will follow them to different venues or to the same venue year after year, so you automatically have a very good opportunity of building up a regular following. If you develop a distinctive style, people will collect your work and comeback season after season looking for your latest designs, which of course is a very good reason to keep your designs fresh.

Other organisers will arrange larger events at a specific venue, often their own, once or twice a year. These can be at garden centres, stately homes, tourist attractions, hotels and shopping centres, or even in town centres. They will normally be two or three day events and will quite often cost £150 a day or more plus VAT. You will definitely require public and product liability insurance before you're allowed to book and any electrical equipment you use will have to have a PAT certificate (portable appliance testing).

Some of these events will be craft and gift fairs which can have pros and cons. It means that you can sell items you have bought in to increase your stock levels, but it also means that your beautiful handmade pieces will be competing directly against mass-market items from China and other countries.

A larger event will attract more people, which means more potential customers. As well as being prepared to speculate more time and money you will also have to have more stock, so that you can make the most of the larger number of people passing your stall.

## School or church fairs

School and church fairs are quite often much shorter events, possibly only two or three hours during the afternoon or in the evening. They can also be midweek, whereas most craft fairs are focused on the weekend. This means that they are easy to fit in around your main schedule. You can quite often leave a large event at about 4pm on Saturday, go and do a small school fair in the evening, and be back at the large event on Sunday morning. Try not to do this too often as it can be very tiring!

Although they are smaller events and they will cost you less rent, they are often quite well attended by people who have every intention of purchasing.

Small fairs are often organised on a seasonal calendar, around Easter, in the summer and for Christmas. Once you are on an organisers list, you will become a regular, doing the same fairs year after year, hopefully attracting a loyal following. Many charity events also fall into the same pattern.

### County shows

County shows, town fairs or big events such as air shows and flower festivals often have a craft marquee as part of the show.

The way this is organised can vary enormously on the type of show. For instance, a local county show can be organised by a committee of local people, while some of the large flower festivals are organised by the Royal Horticultural Society and will normally have their craft marquee organised by one of the Craft Guilds and Associations. For the first type of show, you simply apply as you would with any other event, but for the second you need to be a member of the relevant Crafts Guild.

Most of these shows are held in marquees, hopefully, but not necessarily in good weather, so you should be prepared for the British summer! In fact being prepared is a vital part of making a success of this type of show. Check on the weather forecast and dress for the event, spending an extended time in a marquee can be either very cold or very hot - rarely in the middle. So either have warm clothes and waterproof shoes or have a fan! You also have to take into account that they can be cancelled if the weather is really bad. Some of our recent wet summers have caused havoc with the events calendar and this can have a disastrous affect on your cash flow if you have been depending on the income from a limited number of big events.

Most of the shows will take place over at least two days, many of them can last more and some up to a full week, so you need to make sure that you have plenty of stock.

The rent for this type of show can also vary enormously depending on whether it is a local event or a large national event. Some organisers require you to sign quite long contracts and it is worth reading these to make sure that you know what you are committing yourself to.

One thing to look out for specifically is the clause on cancellation.

There are organisers who will not refund your money even if they cancel the event, which could result in you losing a large upfront investment, possibly the cost of accommodation and of course the loss of the opportunity to sell altogether for that weekend.

You will have to decide if you are willing to take this risk, but it has happened with some very large and very expensive events over recent years when the weather has made it impossible to continue. This is defiantly one of those circumstances when you should read the small print – of course, you always read the contract before signing, don't you!

These larger events are a significant investment in time and money, and only you will be able to decide whether it suits you or not, and at what stage in your business it might suit you.

When they work, large shows can bring in large amounts of money and are very worthwhile investments, but it's probably not a good idea to rely on them totally at first.

### Ideal Home and Fashion Shows

There are also a range of shows that fall into the more professional event range, that specialise in fashion or fashion for the home.

Depending on what your hand knitted designs are, you may find that this more specific type of even is perfect to showcase your work.

You should look around at shows available in your local area and see what is on offer and what you think would suit your work, both in terms of your style of work, the customer that the show targets and the investment required from you.

### Christmas markets

Christmas markets are quite obviously held at Christmas!

They've become very popular in recent years, and they tend to be organised by towns and cities to be held as part of the general Christmas festivities.

Although they do vary from town to town, many of them last a number of weeks and take the form of stalls in the town centre. Sometimes they are the standard market stalls under canvas while some towns set individual wooden huts and others set aside a section of the indoor market or an indoor shopping centre.

Again, if they are outside you have to be prepared for the weather if you decide to do this type of event. Being outside in the winter in Britain can certainly be cold! You will also have to set up and dismantle your stall each day as obviously you cannot leave anything open overnight in the middle of the town centre.

If you are concentrating on Christmas, make sure that you make it easy for the customer to see your designs as a Christmas present. You should also avoid trying to compete head on with the stores. If you knit beautiful jumpers, do you really want to offer the same type of Christmas design jumpers that fill the stores at that time of the year. The majority of customers will just see 'Christmas novelty jumper', they won't be able to see the difference in the quality between your unique handcrafted pieces and the mass produced racks of garments.

Adapt your work to suit the season, but don't follow the fashion slavishly.

If you would like to specialise in the Christmas season, check out my book *How to sell your Christmas Crafts* for some more detailed information.

Again learn from the stores when you are creating potential gifts, in a Christmas market you are competing directly with them. Make it easy for potential customers to buy a ready made gift from you, whether you package them as ready to give gifts, create seasonal 'fun' designs or create sets of your work

## Wedding fairs.

Wedding fairs are very specific events.

Many crafters specialise in creating wedding designs, and although crafts such as jewellery, papercraft or cake making are more obvious candidates for this, you can still adapt knitting to the area of bridal design.

You could create a range of beautiful fine silk knitted stoles and wraps to rival the fashionable but ordinary pashmina.

You could create exquisite ring cushions for the ceremony, or unique table centres or crochet floral bouquets.

Most forms of handcrafting can be adapted to suit the huge wedding market. Invest in some wedding magazines and start to think about how you could create some of the hundreds of items that are now essential for the perfect wedding.

Special orders and bespoke designs are an important part of being a wedding designer.

In a bridal store the bride has to choose from what is available. When she comes to you, she can have a design created specifically for her, including the colours that she wants for her wedding.

This can be a very interesting and lucrative area to specialise in.

Wedding fairs are very often held at wedding venues such as hotels and civic centres. You will find that there is quite a difference in the cost of a wedding fair as opposed to a craft fair. A six-foot table at a craft fair could cost £50, while the same six-foot table in the same room at a wedding fair could cost £150.

You will also need to think specifically about how you design your table for a wedding fair.

The event itself is different. Other stallholders will not be other crafters, they will be professional photographers, wedding dress shops, printers who specialise in wedding stationery, cake designers, suppliers of wedding cars, event organisers, make-up artists and hairdressers.

Many of them will have professional display stands and equipment that they bring from their shops. This doesn't mean that you have to suddenly invest thousands of pounds in professional shopfitting equipment, but it does mean that you have to look very professional.

If you use white cloths make sure that they are a nice heavy quality and of course are spotlessly clean. Although many people choose white, you might decide to stand out from the crowd by using a colour.

Although it is very nice if you can make any sales at the event, doing a wedding fair is mainly about future sales and orders. So it is vital that you have some information that the potential bride can take away with her.

As I mentioned, most of your fellow exhibitors will be wedding professionals. This can have its drawbacks for them, which is potential for you.

Many of them will be manned (or womaned!) by people who work for the company and a lot of them will simply sit behind their stands expecting potential clients to pick up their leaflets. At the other extreme, others will be at the side of their stand shoving their leaflets into any hand that passes, whether the person shows any interest or not.

You will have a chance to be different. Smile at people, engage with them, talk to them. Exhibiting at the wedding fair is all about making connections with people so that they will remember you and so that you will have the opportunity to contact them.

Gathering a list of contacts is vital, because very often, a bride and groom will be looking for ideas for the wedding that can be up to 2 years in the future. So you need to be able to keep in contact with them.

Collect names and addresses and e-mail addresses, and the date of their wedding so that you can target your marketing to suit their timescale.

Don't be afraid of having slightly quirky designs. After all, a bride who simply wants the traditional white and ivory wedding, can buy her items and accessories from hundreds of different places. The bride who wants something different is much more likely to notice you if you don't just display what is expected traditionally.

So if you are offering beautiful angora shrugs for the bride and her bridesmaids, have some in rich burgundy, royal blue and teal, trimmed with vibrant coloured crystals and beads. You might still sell mainly the white, ivory and pastel versions , but the colours will attract attention and will appeal to the bride who can't find what she wants on the high street.

As with all parts of your handmade design business, you can't possibly be all things to all people.

Even if you could produce every style of hand knitting, you can't produce enough of it to sell to everybody. So you may as well specialise in a niche that you enjoy and become a big player in a small niche.

Some of my most successful wedding designs have featured rich colours such as Amethyst, deep ruby reds or rich and vibrant orange.

While not every bride wants to stick to the traditional pale whites and ivories, it's not always easy to find a bridal tiara that features rich purple Amethyst or a dress that has a burgundy bodice.

One of your main selling points is that you are the creator of unique handmade items, rather than a seller of mass produced products.

So have a selection of your fibres, wools, beads and crystals with you at the event. This means that you will be able to show the bride the various colours she could choose from.

Actually knitting at your stand will always attract attention, although you must avoid the pitfall of becoming so engrossed in your work that you risk ignoring the customers!

The ideal situation is being able to get the bride

to place their order for your bespoke handcrafted items, choosing the designs and particularly the colours so that she will have her own unique wedding designs.

Try to get a bride to place her order on the day if you can – after all, you will need time to create her unique items, so understandably your order book is full well into the future!

Brides are prepared to place orders and pay deposits many months and often well over a year into the future in order to get the exact dress/car/cake/venue that they want. So no bride will be put off by your requirement to make a firm booking. In fact it can actually work in your favour, after all, if you are that heavily booked your work must be very good!

## House parties

Selling by party plan at house parties can be a very successful way of selling your handmade designs.

Some of the more traditional party plan has gone a little out of fashion, after all there is only so much kitchen storage that you really want! But that doesn't mean that the idea of party plan is out of date. Far from it, it just means that people are looking for more unusual reasons to have a party.

Unique pieces of hand knitted design are ideal for this. Most women love to have something unique, whether it is a piece of fashion or for their home. Hand knitting is a very easy present to give to others – who doesn't like a new scarf? And you can have enough of a price range to make it comfortable for everybody at the party. Because although some people can quite comfortably afford to spend £100 or £150 or more on a designer garment or bag, in these more economically challenging times there are many others who would be relieved to be able to just spend £10 or £20 without embarrassment.

Once you have started doing house parties, they do have a tendency to feed off themselves, in fact that's the whole idea of a successful party plan business. Someone, preferably two people at the party will book parties of their own and invite different selections of people, which will lead on again to more bookings and more new customers.

Obviously the best way to start, is if you can persuade some of your friends to hold a party for you. But you can also arrange to work with someone who already does party plan with a different product and is willing to let you join them.

You should also advertise the fact that you do parties at every other event that you attend.

There are a few main things you need to do, to create a successful party plan business.

**Make it easy for the host to have a party.**

Create invitations or leaflets that they can hand out to their friends.

People need to know what to expect to see for sale at the party and how much they expect the items to cost, so that they have an idea of the price ranges. They also need to know when and where it is. It's a good idea to put some photos of your hand knitting onto the invitation and if you have a website put the address on so that they can go and have a look at the type of handmade designs that you have for sale. And do emphasise that it is handmade, by you rather than just mass produced and available at the market.

**Make it worthwhile for the host to have a party.**

She will be going to quite a lot of trouble and some expense, providing wine and nibbles at least for her guests, as well as putting the time in to arrange the party. So it has to be worth her while.

You can decide on the exact style of your incentive, but generally it will be something like a percentage of the value of your total sales in the evening to be spent on her own order. The percentage is up to you, but is normally somewhere between 10% and 20%. You could also decide to give a bonus for each person that books a further party, or a special offer only available to the organiser on the evening. The more creative you can be, the more successful you should be in booking future parties. After all, people are more likely to book a party of their own if they feel it's going to be worthwhile to them.

**Make it easy to set up your party.**

For both your sake and your host's sake, you don't want to spend two hours setting up your display! Design an easy and time efficient way of carrying and setting out your range. You have a limited amount of time and space when doing a house party, so don't try to take every design you've ever made. Decide from your experience, what your bestsellers are and make sure that you have them together with enough variety for people to have a choice, but not so much that it overwhelms them.

**Make it interesting for the host and her guests**.

Don't just put your hand knitting out and expect it to sell itself. Don't just stand in a corner like a wallflower. Give a short talk that explains something about your hand knitting, what makes it special, what makes it different, do you use natural fibres. Do you make spin your own fibre? Are your garments machine washable? Do you offer them in a large range of sizes and colours?

Give them an idea of the price range. Talk about how you can design special pieces for them. How jumpers and jackets can be made in a size and length to suit, because each one is handmade.

**Make it easy for the guests to make a purchase**.

Most party plan businesses rely on people placing an order and receiving it at a later date and obviously if you are creating garments to order, there will have to be a delivery time for special orders.

But I always think it's a good idea if you can create a selection of my handmade items for them to take away on the night, in the same way as you have a range of items for people to buy on the day at a fair.

When I do take special orders, I prefer to either

deliver or post the piece out to the customer directly rather than expecting the host of the party to do the deliveries for me.

Finally make it easy and worthwhile for the guests to book a party of their own. The life blood of a party plan business is to continually book new parties. If you book one party from each party that you do, your business will stay level. If you book two parties from each party you do your business will grow. But if you don't book any parties, your business will die.

### Markets

Many towns hold regular markets. Some of these are general markets, some of them are farmers markets, and some of them are craft markets. Which type you might decide to take a stall at is entirely up to you. Different markets suit different crafters, but there are some general rules that apply to any of them.

Most market organisers will supply the stalls, which are normally a metal framework covered by a (mostly) waterproof canvass. They will also normally supply the table top for you to set your product out on. You will have to supply your own covers, and of course you won't have electricity in most cases.

Markets take place on every day of the week. Some towns have a weekly market, whereas others are held on every day of the week. Many market traders have a weekly route around their local towns, setting up shop every morning in the next town. As a crafter it is highly unlikely that you will follow that pattern as you need time to create your product, so you would probably only do two or maybe three regular days a week.

Some of the indoor markets have space allocated for a specialist Craft fair that they hold once a month. Although these are held in markets, they do follow more the pattern of the craft fair. You will have a 6 foot table as your stall and you probably will have an electrical supply.

Markets, whether indoor or outside, are very open areas, with the public milling around rather than people who have chosen to come into a craft fair.

This means that you can have a much wider range of potential customers, but it also means that you have to be more aware of the risk of shoplifters. Make sure that any expensive pieces of hand knitting are out of the way of sticky fingers – both literally and figuratively – a beautiful delicate alpaca throw will be ruined if someone picks it up while eating their fish and chips. So take care of your stock and take care of your cash.

If you are planning on doing many markets, it is worth joining the National Market Traders Federation in the UK, membership of which gives you public and product liability insurance, as well as many other benefits.

### Talks to social and church groups
There are many groups who are constantly looking for people to give talks at their monthly meetings.

Obviously, many of the people who will give talks will require some payment to cover their costs.

If you are able to take a selection of your designs with you, and have them available for their members to purchase, then you can offer to give the talk without charge.

You are taking the risk that you will give the talk and not take any money, but personally, I have never had this happen. In fact, many of these events can be extremely lucrative.

I always give a gift to the organisation that they can use as a raffle prize, sometimes on the night, sometimes with a raffle to be held at a later date, it's their choice. As a designer of unique handcrafted items, you can give a gift that is worth a lot more than it costs you to produce.

Many members of such groups are members of more than one, so as always, do make sure that everyone has your contact details. As with party plan, you will find that you make bookings from bookings.

Again, as with party plan, make it easy to set up your display.

For both your sake and the group's sake, you don't want to spend two hours setting up your stand! They will often only have access to the hall about half an hour before the start of their meeting. Normally, they will deal with group business, such as reading the minutes, first and then hand the rest of the meeting over to you.

You will have to be able to set up your display

quickly and quietly. You will also need to be able to pack it away quickly once the meeting is over.

Design an easy and time efficient way of carrying and setting out your range, don't try to take every design you've ever made. You will also have to be flexible about how you set out your display a

s you will not always know beforehand what type of tables that they will supply.

Decide from your experience what your bestsellers are and make sure that you have them, together with enough variety for people to have a choice, but not so much that it overwhelms them. You'll find over time that your bestsellers vary from venue to venue and event type to event type. Keep a record of what you sell so that you can see any patterns that emerge.

Make it interesting for the group, you are there to give a talk after all. Don't just put your hand knitting out and expect it to sell itself, selling anything is supposed to be a bonus at this type of event. Give a short talk that explains something about your work, what makes it special, what makes it different, do you use recycled fibres or natural yarns, or do you dye your own fibres.

For this type of talk, you can get more personal, because they are not just interested in buying your hand knitted designs, they are interested in what drew you into designing in the first place. How did you learn? How long have you been knitting? Where do you get your design inspiration? What made you decide to set up business?

Give them an idea of the price range, show how you can create a whole look for themselves or for their home. Talk about how you can design special pieces for them - soft furnishings to compliment a colour palate, an outfit for a special event. How garments can be made at a size to suit, because each one is handmade.

Once you have finished your talk, which you should keep to about 20 to 30 minutes, be prepared for a rush! This is not a leisurely day long craft fair, everybody wants to be served within about 15 minutes before they rush off to get a bus, meet someone who's giving them a lift, or just get home!

These talks can take place during the day or in the evenings and at any time of the week, depending on what type of group you are talking to. So you can fit quite a number into your calendar. They are often booked over a year in advance as the social secretary arranges the plan for the year.

## Demonstrations

Demonstrations are a great way of selling. It shows people that you do actually know what you're doing. They love seeing how something is made, that it is actually a handcrafted piece of hand knitting created in front of them, although of course with most pieces of knitting, you won't be able to make a bespoke piece on the day.

If you can set aside some space to demonstrate you will normally be able to gather a crowd to your stall. Some organisers will give you extra space if you are willing to demonstrate, because they know that this is a draw for the public. When your craft is knitting, it's important to make a show of it if you are going to demonstrate, otherwise it's too easy to look as if you are just filling in time behind your stand!

Set up a display of some of the yarns that you use, you could set aside some times during the show - that you advertise of course - where you will actually teach the basics of knitting. To go with that, you could create some starter kits with a basic instruction sheet and pattern, some knitting needles and yarn. In fact, the knitting kits and some of your own designer patterns could become a major part of your business.

There are also times when you will be asked to simply go and demonstrate your craft. This can be in a craft store, where they want to sell the idea of knitting and therefore the yarns, needles and patterns. It can be at a school or youth club, where they would like you to teach others how to knit, and in this case, your knitting starter kits could be very successful.

One of the benefits of this is that it creates an image for you as an expert in your field. And as well as leading to work demonstrating or teaching it can also lead to sales and special orders for your hand knitting.

### Be prepared to expand

So as you can see, there are many different ways of reaching out to your customer in face-to-face situations.

Most people do start out with local craft fairs, but as you begin to do these craft shows, you will find that other opportunities open up to you and you should always make sure that you are prepared for the opportunity.

Many organisers arranging new events, or looking for new stallholders for their well-established events, will visit other craft fairs looking for fresh ideas and new designers.

Other organisers looking for speakers for their regular meetings or craftspeople who are willing to come to their workplaces, callcentres or nursing homes and set up stall for a few hours, will visit craft fairs to look for suitable ideas.

Some of these organisers will actually stop to talk to you, but others prefer to simply pick up your business card or leaflet and call you at a later date. So obviously it is very important to have a business card or leaflet on your stall.

If you do a number of events, prepare a leaflet that lists them all so that people can follow you around. Regular customers are very valuable and they will also recommend you to their friends.

Include your contact details on this leaflet, your business name, your phone number, your e-mail address and website but be very careful about putting your geographical address. If you work from home, you are effectively giving people a list of dates when your home will be empty!

If you would like to do party plan or talks, add this to your leaflet. You can also produce a more detailed leaflet about your party plan arrangements, which you can hand out to people if they ask about it.

The important thing is to remember that you are now running a business and you must give yourself every opportunity to reach new customers, enter new markets, develop new products and new ideas and grow your business.

Even if you do want to keep your business small so that it will fit in with the rest of the commitments in your life – and there's nothing wrong with that – you should still widen your opportunities to sell as much as possible. If you rely on a single craft fair organiser or a single market, your business will be devastated if that outlet ceases trading for any reason.

And of course, if you have your sights set on creating a major brand – and a lot of big brands have started at craft fairs and markets – you will need to look for every opportunity to grow and develop your company.

# What's your product?

Knitting is a craft that can be turned to many different product ranges and it's important to decide what you intend to do when you begin to think about turning your hobby into a business.

When you are knitting for yourself, your friends and family, and even when you are producing some knitted items for school or church fairs or your local charity shop, you can happily mix up a whole range of styles and products.

Jumpers for yourself, baby clothes for your family and friends, scarves and hats for the church fund raising, knitted toys for the school fair and small blankets for the charity shop.

But once you want to turn your hobby into a business you have to start thinking about your knitting as a product range and you will have to focus your attention on exactly what you want to produce.

Each different type of product will require a different type of marketing, a different way of displaying it at your events, a different set of questions when you are choosing an event, different pricing, packaging choices, even different decisions about storing and transporting your stock.

As a basic guide, these are some of the things you will want to take into account for the different type of products you can product with hand knitting. I'm sure you'll think of more as you begin to concentrate on what your decisions are and what they will demand of you once your hobby becomes a business.

Part of your decision will be based on what level of pricing you want to pitch your designs at. If you think you will be selling at events that are very price conscious – and some are! – then you will want to choose a range that you can product quickly and in reasonably priced yarn. There is no point in spending many hours on a design when the price you can charge will only just cover the cost of the yarn.

## Baby Knitting

When you're knitting for babies and young children you have to take into account that many of your customers will be grandparents and in many cases this means that they are looking for more traditional designs.

Although you will need to create your designs in blue and pink, also allow for the fact that many people will be buying gifts for the birth of a baby, and sometimes they won't know whether it's going to be a boy or girl – so make sure that you have some designs in gender neutral colours such as the obvious white, but also yellows, oranges, greens and creams.

You could also add some more vibrant colours to your collection – they may not be as popular in general, but you would be offering a product in a niche market and may well be able to sell many more bootees in bright purple, pillerbox red and electric blue when you are the only one offering them.

When you are a small producer – as all crafters are – it can be much more profitable to concentrate on a niche market than trying to compete with all the stores, websites and catalogues. You can create a name for your business and use that to grow.

You should also make sure that you have a selection of bootees, hats, mittens, all-in-ones, crib blankets and baby shawls to give you the best chance of attracting the impulse purchase, as most of your items will be bought as gifts.

You will need to be able to give your customers advice on the a size of your items in terms of the babies age – the normal guides are Newborn, 0-3 months, 3-6 months , 6-9  months, 9-12 months, and 12-18 months, but you might also want to do some of your designs for premature babies.

As well as putting the age guide on, you should be able to give some guidance as to the weight of the baby, especially in the smaller sizes – people will ask you!

The choice of yarn is also important for this market. Of course it is important in whatever designs you decide to produce, but if you are knitting baby items you should take into account the delicate skins that will be wearing your items, and you should make sure that your potential customers know that you have thought about it. Advertise the fact if you only use natural fibres, tell people if your items can be put in the washing machine, busy mothers need easy care garments.

When you're arranging your little jumpers, cardigans and all-in-ones, have them in order of size so that it is easier for you or your customer to find the right one – of course you will have to have tags firmly attached to identify them – I find that a simple tag with a string or wool loop works well, fastened to the garment with a small safety pin – it can look very classy and doesn't damage your valuable knitting. Of course, you will need to continually rearrange your stock – some people manage to get them into the most awful mess!

Try to avoid the temptation to put all your work out at the same time. Have a sign to let people know that you have other sizes available. Most people will happily ask if you have a design in the size they want and this has a number of advantages.

- It helps you keep your work clean and safe if you can keep it individually wrapped in your undertable stock room
- People are more likely to 'buy now' if they

think the supply is limited.
- You can avoid the image of 'pile them high, sell them cheap'
- You can interact with a potential customer when they ask if you have the size they want, which gives you the opportunity to show that you have hats and bootees to match.

Finally, taking into account that many of your items will be bought as gifts, you can easily increase the perceived value of your work with your packaging. Make the effort to source some packaging that is suitable for babies – you can probably find a stationary or greeting card supplier either locally or on-line.

Take the time to wrap the beautiful little garments in tissue paper and present them in a gift bag.

It doesn't have to add a lot to your costs but it can add a great deal to your image and to the price range that you present your designs at. You will never be able to beat the prices that the stores and supermarkets sell at, and you can only produce a limited number of items, so find outlets that will enable you to sell them at a price that is worth your work.

## Toys

If you are going to sell knitted toys there are regulations to take into account.

Toys must be safe – obviously - and different

countries have their own rules and regulations about items that are aimed at children or can be seen as children's toys. You cannot simply say that they are not intended for children under 14 and avoid the law.

In the UK, toys that are aimed at children under the age of 14, are required to have a CE logo. The Toy Safety Directive 2011 covers handmade products that look like toys, even if you have specified that they are for decorative use.

The only exception to this is for Christmas/novelty designs.

You can self certify your designs and www.conformance.co.uk ( a specialist consultancy specialising in all areas of product safety) have packs that are designed to help home toy-makers meet the legal requirements of the Toy Safety Directive.

In the USA Congress passed the Consumer Product Safety Act in 2008 and this states that any products intended for children under 12 must be tested and certified by a qualified lab, although they do have allowances for a small batch manufacturer, but you have to register.

The laws are constantly evolving and you should do some research when you are thinking of adding knitted toys to your range.

Of course, it goes without saying that you should take care in sourcing any of your components for toys – such as eyes, plastic noses or the stuffing you use. The best way to do this is to purchase your components from reputable suppliers who can give you details of the safety testing that their parts have been through.

You will also have to produce labels stating your contact details and what materials you have used in the manufacture of your toys – yes, you are manufacturing them, even when you only knit a few dozen.

But you should see this as a positive rather than a problem. Producing labels for your knitted designs makes them look more professional and therefore more valuable. It also gives you the chance to advertise your business to everyone who receives some of your work as a gift.

You can create a small number of beautiful and collectable designs that you will sell for higher prices – don't be scared of valuing your expertise and setting your prices high to attract the customers who will pay for your work.

At the other end of the scale you can create small, quickly produced finger puppets and simple little characters that will attract the attention – and pocket money – of the younger visitors to a craft fair. It's worth creating some designs in the colours of your local sports team. Be careful not to use their actual logo or copy designs that they produce - you don't want to get involved in any copyright disputes – but no one can stop you knitting little characters in black and white, red and white or blue and white stripes.

Although the most obvious thing to consider when making toys are the designs for teddies and stuffed characters, you can also knit unique outfits for dolls and either sell them with a doll or on their own. I find it best to have both – some beautifully dressed dolls and then other outfits that your customers can collect.

You can choose to knit for baby dolls or teenage fashion dolls, but you should try and produce outfits for the popular sizes of doll available in the main market. That means that more children will want to buy your outfits for their own dolls at home. If you are producing outfits for dolls, it can also be worthwhile adding matching accessories such as headbands, hats, scarves or hairclips for the child to wear so she and her doll can be coordinated.

## Christmas knitting

Christmas designs and novelty products are the two areas that are exempt from the Toy Safety Directive, so you might prefer to concentrate your work in this area if you are worried about rules and regulations.

The Christmas market is huge, many of the big retailers can stand or fall on the success of their Christmas season, if you'd like to learn more about selling Christmas crafts I have written a book dedicated to that area *'How to sell your Christmas Crafts'*.

People love to have unique, handcrafted decorations for Christmas rather than relying on the mass produced items offered in the big stores.

Christmas knitting can cover quite a range of

knitting projects. The obvious ones are tree and table decorations and festive jumpers, but you can spread your net wide with a seasonal theme.

Many people buy knitted items as gifts – the hats, scarves and mittens that many people find in their Christmas stocking.

All of them can be purchased from the local supermarket or department store, but you can offer something unique – you can even offer to personalise designs. Embroider a name on the Christmas stocking to make it an heirloom item that is brought out year after year.

If you do decide to personalise your designs, make sure that you have a clear sign on your stand to let people know.

You will also have to decide if you are going to make a charge for personalisation or if it will be part of the product and whether you will do it in a simple style on the day or whether the items will be made to order.

Do remember to take a substantial deposit if not full payment for personalised orders and make sure that you have the correct spelling for the name – they vary so much! You will also have to allow for postage and packaging if you are going to send the orders out.

You can have some of the more popular names available to buy 'off the shelf', but remember that you could be left with quite a stock of unsold items if you decide to pre-make.

You might want to have an on-line outlet for your work if you decide to take this route, to allow you access to a larger audience.

If you are going to concentrate your efforts on the Christmas market, make sure that your whole image follows through with this.

Decorate your stall with tinsel and Christmas lights, I find it a good selling point if I use Christmas gift bags as packaging, then the gift is ready to give

## Accessories

Knitting accessories can be fun and can cover quite a wide range of designs, from very traditional to fun and funky. Scarves can be traditional woollen designs, funky eyelash fibres or luxurious, highly decorative lace designs in silk.

Whatever your mix of accessories – scarves, boleros, shawls, hats, gloves or mittens, hair bands or slides – you must make sure that you have a style running through the whole collection. Don't be tempted to mix colourful, long striped acrylic scarves with delicate lace designs in fine mohair – you will undermine the sales of both types of work.

You must always keep in mind how the potential customers will see your stand, and confusing them with a muddle of styles and prices that don't work together will just mean that most potential customers will pass you by. So rather than attracting more sales by offering items at all price points, you will actually end up with fewer sales as you confuse people and stop them looking at all.

When you are concentrating on accessories, it's a good idea to co-ordinate your colour schemes on your shopfront so that people can see the designs that will work together and create sets. Try and display some sets together on your stands or on a small mannequin.

This is one of the areas of knitting when you can follow fashion, the garments are relatively quick to make and you should have a fast turnover, so your fashion colours shouldn't stay around too long.

## Bags

Bags – especially handbags and flight bags - have become so fashionable in recent years – and so expensive! So if you can create a following in this area of hand knitting you can create your own, unique, collectable fashion brand. After all, every big name started somewhere.

Your bags will have the added advantage of being truly limited in number and collectable. In fact you could decide to create limited editions, labelling and numbering each one in a collection. People love to know they've got something special, that they are part of an elite group.

If you don't want to follow the high end designer path, there are still lots of designs that you can create in this field.

Evening bags, vintage designs, glamour and glitz with lurex and beading,

And you can move away from handbags altogether. Craft bags, purses, phone and tablet sleeves, computer bags, make up bags, shopping bags, tote bags, beach bags and of course - knitting bags.

Use some tissue paper to pack out some of your bags as they do in the stores. A bag always looks more 'real' if it is padded out and looks more like a bag in use.

There is also a rule that works for most things that you want to sell. If you want to position your designs at a higher price, have fewer on display, allowing each one to shine out like an individual jewel on your stand.

### Home decor

Designing hand knitted home decor can open up your choice of designs.

You can create designs for the living room, the bedroom, the kitchen or the bathroom. But it is very important to decide what you are going to concentrate on and then focus your work.

Again, you should create a style that is identifiably yours, otherwise you will alienate potential customers across the board.

So if you want to create elegant, traditional aran design cushions, throws, lampshades, baskets and rugs, don't confuse your display by adding a few brightly coloured tea cosy's, oven gloves and coasters.

Decide on your image and your target customer and make the most of it, displaying your designs so that they attract those customers.

You should also choose your events to suit the

work you will be offering. Fun and funky accessories for the kitchen, bathroom or office can be created quickly, and often with inexpensive yarns, which means that you can afford to price them at impulse purchase prices.

Highly detailed  cushion covers, afghans and rugs take a lot longer to create and you will be working with more expensive and a larger quantity of yarn for each design, so you will have to be able to charge more money for your work. You can also add some lower cost items to your collection so that you can still attract the impulse buy and small gift, by designing covers for flowerpots, penpots, table mats and coasters, but you will still need to choose events that target customers with a higher disposable income, and you will probably want to be able to take orders for customised designs.

## Fashion

Fashion – by its very nature – has to be in fashion!

But hand knitting takes time and you can't copy the model of some of the stores that have items from the red carpet and the pages of a magazine to the shop floor in a matter of days or, at most, a couple of weeks.

You will have to set your sights at seasonal fashions rather than the absolute cutting edge of the fashion world.

It's also worth remembering that things go out of fashion as well, so don't make too many pieces of a design for your stock. There's nothing less valuable than last year's high fashion.

Try to find the middle ground, a trend that will probably stick around for a year or two at least, you can always keep it up to date by adding the latest trendy colour to your range.

Follow the lead of some of the biggest fashion names. They have their latest, brightest colours and designs on show, but they always have their basics as well, the designs and colours that sell year after year.

## Traditional garments

There are many traditional forms of knitting, the most famous are the designs from Shetland, Scandinavia, Aran, Fair Isle and the fisherman's jumpers that were created in fishing villages around Britain as well as many traditional designs from around Europe.

These designs are often complex, taking skill and knowledge of the time-honoured stitches and patterns used in the designs.

It is a specialised market and customers are willing to pay you for the time and skill involved in creating these heirloom pieces.

If this is your speciality it's worth taking the time to create brochures and to let people know that your garments are very special and not available in the mass market. You will often take orders for such pieces, possibly incorporating the initials of the customer into the design.

## Luxury designs

The pashmina introduced the idea of knitted luxury garments into the public's mind and there's now a large market for exclusive woollen, cashmere, alpaca and silk designs.

Hand knitting is no longer only seen as unwanted Christmas presents!

Concentrating on luxury pieces gives you the opportunity to work with beautiful yarns. You could decide only to work with natural fibres sourced close to home. You might be able to work with a supplier who spins their own yarn, or who uses natural dyes in small batches.

You could work with recycled sari silks, natural cotton, pure cashmere or alpaca.

If you are creating luxury garments created in expensive yarns, you have to be able to price them to take into account the cost of the materials and the time you invest in each piece. But you also need to price them at a level that indicates that you are creating exclusive, luxury items.

A hand knitted cashmere sweater should be priced in the hundreds. You can only produce a limited number, so you will have to find events that will attract customer willing to pay for your work.

Your presentation – from setting out your display to the packaging that you use – will have to set the tone and let your customers know that they are investing in a luxury hand crafted item.

## Knitted jewellery

There are a number of other ranges you can choose to create. Some of them may well work in with another range, while some can stand alone.

Knitted jewellery and hair ornaments can be a main range, you could concentrate on selling at school fetes, or in the craft marquee of town and country fairs where children are always looking for small items they can buy with pocket money.

At the other end of the design scale, you could create the same type of designs in silk and mohair with lurex, crystal beads and pearls, and concentrate on the wedding and school prom market.

You can create novelty items - cup cakes as pin cushions, rockets as pencil cases, bunting, dog coats, flowers or fancy dress designs.

The craft of knitting can be turned to almost anything, so you should find something that you really like and concentrate on that. After all, you don't want to spend hours knitting things you don't like.

# What's your style?

You probably haven't thought about having a style before, you just hand knit for your own pleasure, probably as gifts for friends and family, maybe even for orders from friends and work colleagues.

Most small design businesses start off like this, almost by accident.

But all along you will have been developing a style, even if it's not well-defined yet.

Now is the time to think about it.

When you decide to take the step to selling your hand knitting, which you have or are about to if you're reading this book, you need to start developing a style of your own.

No business, no matter how large it is, can be all things to all people and when you're creating a small business based on hand crafting, that is even more true.

So rather than trying to do everything, concentrate on one thing and do it really well.

## Focus your attention

As we discussed in the last chapter, knitting is a skill that can be used to create an almost infinite variety of items.

The obvious starting place for most people is the idea of wearable objects such as jumpers, scarves, hats and gloves, and even that gives you a huge variety to choose from.

But look at any of the knitting magazines, pattern books and the amount of knitted products in the stores.

You might knit toys and dolls clothes, fashionable handbag, cases for smart phones and tablets, cushion covers, afghans and throws, kitchen or bathroom accessories – the choice goes on and on.

If you're knitting for yourself and your friends you've probably created almost every type of piece on the list, but you're now running a business and it's very important to focus so that your potential customer knows what to expect from you.

There are many interpretations of style, and it isn't limited to choosing to knit cushions or scarves for your business.

I don't mean that you should only make cream jumpers, or one design of computer case, although that could work,  the most famous designer names have very strong, individual styles.

Sonia Rykiel, is famous for inventing inside out stitching, no-hem and 'un-lined' pieces.

The Italian based fashion house Missoni, is famous for unique designs in colourful patterns such as stripes, abstract florals and geometric patterns in a rainbow of colours.

Irish designer Tim Ryan is known for sexy, sophisticated knitwear. The self taught designer uses pure wools and silk yarns highlighted with lots of lurex and glitter.

London based designer Timothy James Andrew designs chunky knits decorated with colourful pom poms to create, fun, structural garments.

You can find many knitwear designers who have created a very strong look in their work and as long as you have a strong image and style, you can develop this over a number of different products. Take a look at some of the fashion houses, Chanel and Yves St Laurant are known for their couture collections but that doesn't stop them using their unique style and image to create collections of handbags, jewellery and accessories

So, look at the hand knitting you make and decide what the main elements are.

Do you work with natural fibres, chunky yarns, or silk?

Do you use recycled yarns, incorporate fabric in your designs or add lurex details in the main design?

Do you add beadwork or leather fringing to your designs?

Do you specialise in beautiful, dainty handbags or large funky tote bags?

Do you work in subtle pastels, a rainbow of brights or a palette of creams?

Once you start to think about it, you'll find that

you do actually have a style of your own, a style that you can develop and become known for.

When you've decided on your main style and what you feel you want to concentrate on, you can begin to make decisions about what you think your hand knitting design and image should be.

At this stage it's probably worth discarding some of the designs that really don't fit into your new design style.

As we decided earlier, you can't be all things to all people, so now is the time to think about who your target customer is.

If your range is going to be fun and funky, aimed at the young and fashionably young at heart, you'd be wasting your time and investment by adding in a few finely knitted cashmere pieces.

Worse, you'd be diluting your image, confusing potential customers and alienating both sets. Think back to your market research. If a store mixed up bright fun throwaway fashion T-shirts with sensible expensive shoes, they would put off both potential customer groups.

The fun and fashionable would see the sensible shoes and be put off. The more mature ladies looking for sensible shoes, would see the funky T-shirts and also walk past!

So it's best to drop the items that lie far outside your central style. They will just confuse your image and damage the overall look of your stand.

Focus on creating a whole collection of designs that will look like they come from the same designer rather than having a mix and not match approach that will end up looking home-made rather than handmade.

## Who is your target customer

The best way of creating this collection is the way that big marketing companies go about it.

Decide who is your target customer is and design for her.

You build up a picture of the person you think will be buying your hand knitting.

What sort of age might she be?

Which of those fashion shops would she be buying in?

Will she be keeping up with the latest trends or going for the classics?

Will she be buying for her daughters as well as herself?

You don't want to be too rigid. After all you do want to sell as much of your work as possible, but it does help focus your mind if you have a target customer to think about as you're planning.

## Creating your brand

Your image doesn't finish with your hand knitting design.

When you are designing and deciding on your target customer, think about how you will present your designs.

What name will you give your new collection. People love brands, and you have to decide on a name that you will put on your business cards and your leaflets. It can be your own name or an adaptation of your name or something completely different.

For instance, someone called Sarah Jane could call her new hand knitting business Sarah Jane hand knitting, Sarah Jane Designs, SJ hand knitting, SJ Alpaca hand knitting. Or she could pick something entirely different - Cotton Creations, Cuddle Toys, KnitWit Bags!

A brand name gives your customers something to follow. If they see a list of exhibitors at a craft fair, they will know whether you will be there. They'll be able to tell their friends who to look for. It's much better if they can say, look for KnitWit Bags, rather than the tall girl with dark hair!

## Designing your logo

Now that you've got this far, you have a knitting style and a business name, you can begin to think about the image of your entire business.

What will your colour scheme be?

What sort of font will you use for your new business name. This is the point at which your business name becomes your logo.

Writing exactly the same word in a number of different fonts and using different colours will create different images.

Try this out on your computer. Pick a simple name and repeat it a number of times on the page. Then use a different font each time. Once you print it out, you will see what a difference it makes.

Again learn from the professionals. They spend millions of pounds making slight alterations to their logos. It might seem a terrible waste of money, but the way a brand is written affects the way we see them, and how we think of their services or their products.

Cotton Creations , written in a traditional script font will give the impression of being traditional and elegant. Pictures of elegant casuals and cruise wear will spring to mind as soon as someone reads your name.

But if you want to attract the more funky customer to your funky hand knitting, then you want to choose a font and a style that will show them that you have something different to offer right from the very start. And that start comes with your logo.

Now you're really beginning to get somewhere.

You know what kind of hand knitting you're going to design and who you're going to sell it to. And you know what your company image looks like now that you've developed your business name and your logo. You're beginning to feel like a real business.

None of these things have to cost you a fortune or even take that long to create, but it makes the difference between selling some home-made hand knitting at a church fete and selling your unique handmade designs at craft fairs and other events.

Having formed this idea of your style, you will find it easier to make other decisions about your new business.

Deciding what your colour scheme is.

What colour covers you will have for your table.

What type of packaging you will choose.

What type of promotions you will run.

It will even help focus your mind so that you can decide where you will sell your handmade designs.


## Unique Selling Point

Otherwise known as your USP, every business should have a unique selling point, but what is it!

It's what sets you, your business and your hand knitting, apart from other people. It's what your business stands for. It's what's important to you. It is also back to the point of not trying to be everything to everyone.

Working out what your USP is can help you focus your mind on what you actually want to do and how you want to be seen.

Okay, at its simplest, you want to sell your handmade knitted designs.

But why do you want to make a business out of your hand knitting?

Is one of your aims to be able to get away from the mass production that we see nowadays?

Do you love creating something totally unique, each piece is being a part of your own personality?

Do you want each of your intricate fair isle designs to be a unique work of art? Something collectable and valued as a piece of artwork as much as a piece of hand knitting

Do you concentrate on ethical sourcing of your yarns?

Or do you focus on recycling in your design work?

Take some time about your USP.

It's a worthwhile process personally as well as for your business. It means that you will be concentrating on why you have started selling your hand knitting.

What do you love about knitting, what do you love about the materials that you use? Are you a fibre junky?

What are your passions?

After all, this is not just a job. You have taken the decision to start a creative business of your own, and it's very exciting! If it's not exciting, it might be time to rethink things because it takes quite a lot of work, and you'll probably find yourself knitting late into the night sometimes, so it definitely needs to be something that you love doing. And that is the best part about this whole process - being able to make money from something you love doing.

It means that you never really go to work!

# Presenting Yourself

The design of your stand will depend on the type of products you are going to sell. Obviously you will need rails and mannequins if you are selling garments that need to be displayed as they are worn, but for many types of knitted product you will be dealing with the same type of display requirements as many other crafts.

### Setting out your stall

When you're selling face-to-face, whether it's at markets, country fairs, school or church events, craft fairs, wedding shows or house parties -your main display counter will be a table.

Normally a 6' x 2' table, and you have to be prepared to adapt to different sizes, because unless you use your own table you will be taking potluck. Some will be narrow, some wide, some hotels will even put out roundtables (although luckily not many!)

Even if you book a space at a large professional

exhibition, you will still normally start with a table inside your booth. You can move on to a display of shelves and glass cabinets if you are going to be concentrating your business on exhibition space, but you won't begin your career with that type of investment.

So - a 6 foot table. How do you turn that into an attractive shopfront?

You need four basic things:

A cover

Height

Display stands.

Lighting

## The cover.

The cover is quite straightforward. It wants to be big enough to cover your table to the floor. It looks very amateurish to have it hanging in midair. You want to create your own space, and while the top of the table is your selling space, under the table is your store room and you don't want to leave the store room wide open for the public to see!

You can use standard tablecloths or sheets if you need to but it's worth setting yourself up properly in the first place.

Find a fabric shop – you can find them on-line as well as on the hightstreet - preferably one that sells upholstery and curtain fabric and buy some sheeting.

Sheeting is wide enough to cover the top and front of your stand and you can buy enough length to stretch past each end of the table so that you can create a tidy corner with the aid of some hospital corners and safety pins. (For those who don't know, a hospital corner is a way of tidily folding the bedsheets!)

You will also have a choice of colours. The colour of your cloth will be the basis of your whole look and is a major part of your overall style.

Crisp white – (which needs to be kept spotlessly clean)

Elegant black or Goth Black

Rich burgundy.

Cool blue

Funky yellow

Pretty pink

Whatever colour you choose you will want the rest of your display to work with it, so it is a very important decision. Don't be tempted to grab the first thing you find and think that will do. If you don't put some thought into it at this stage you will end up replacing your covers quite quickly which is an unnecessary expense.

It's also worth buying some extra fabric so that you can use this to cover any extra boxes that you will use as stands.

If you can't find exactly the colour you've decided on, buy white sheeting and dye it to the colour you want. If you do choose this method make sure that you prepare more fabric than you think you'll need. There will be times when you book more space at a fair and you'll need cloths for at least a 12ft display.

## Height

A flat 6 x 2 table with hand knitting just lying on it will look - well flat!

Boring and uninteresting. Dull.

You get the idea? It will look amateurish and apart from anything else, you're limiting your display space

Think back to that shopping centre. Did any of the shops have their designs lying flat on the bottom of the window display? No! They have hundreds of pounds worth of display stands layered up on beautiful shelving to show everything off.

Your version doesn't need cost hundreds of pounds, there are lots of ways that you can create the same sort of effect. Be creative.

Height adds interest, it adds variation, it adds space.

One of the easiest ways to add height is to unpack the boxes you carry everything in, turn them upside down and cover them in smaller cloths that match your main table cover.

If you do use this method, then your choice of storage box becomes a bit more important. You want to select suitable sizes, not too big and not too small, and possibly a variety of sizes. You also want to choose boxes with flat bases, so that they will create good, stable shelving.

One of the best types of box is a sturdy cardboard case that fruit and vegetables are delivered in to the greengrocers and supermarkets. They are strong, often have good handle slots for carrying, they stack on top of one another, they have flat bases and they're free!

Most types of hand knitted product will be quite light but bulky, so you will probably need quite a few boxes as well as some large bags to carry your designs.

Once you drape your cloth over the boxes, no one will guess how humble your beautiful shelving really is.

## Display stands

Now that you have the main bones of your counter, you can add even more height.

The type of height you will need depends on the type of hand knitting you've made.

If you have lots of scarves or shawls, you might want to create some tall framework that you can use to drape your work over.

Other styles of hand knitting require other types of display. After all, you will need some way of displaying your individual star pieces of hand knitting

You will see some people selling their work all just laid out flat on a flat table. But this makes nothing of the individual pieces and it tends to looks amateurish. It does have its place, for instance if you want to give the impression of selling very low value pieces. And I say the impression because these aren't often sold at a low price, they are just perceived as cheap and sometimes the mass produced, low quality items can actually cost more money than genuine hand knitted designs created in beautiful natural yarns.

This style of display, if it's done deliberately, is done to create the image of pile it high, sell it cheap and can work well in a flea market or car boot sale or even a school table top sale where you want to create the impression of affordability.

But in most cases you will want to create a better image for your handcrafted work. Whatever materials you work with, you have put time and skill into the piece and you want to show it off at its best.

If you make jumpers or shrugs, you probably want to use some busts to display them. If you make bags you should fill some of them with tissue to show them as working bags, like the departments stores do, and display them on some form of shelving at different heights.

If you knit soft toys you will also want some form of shelving to create a variety in the heights on your stand.

If you do sell garments and want to use garments rails or mannequins, do remember that they have to fit inside the space you have booked and paid for.

The space between tables is there for both you and your neighbouring stall holder to be able to get in and out from behind the stall, it is not space for you to fill up with your stock. No one likes space invaders and you will make yourself very unpopular if you do encroach on someone else's space. The organiser will also take you to task for it. So if you want to have your table and a garment rail, book and pay for extra space. The alternative is to ask if you can use your own smaller table, allowing space for the rail within your original six foot space.

Although most craft fair stands are six foot, you can of course book a double space to give you more shop room, and some organisers allow you to book varying sizes, although with some it will be a multiple of the standard six foot, so twelve or even eighteen if you are feeling very adventurous.

I will normally have a twelve foot stand, eighteen can be quite difficult to manage, especially if you have to work on your own at times, and of course you have to have a lot of stock to fill the space and make the outlay worthwhile.

## Lighting

It's very tempting to ignore lighting, especially when you are first starting out, but that is a mistake.

The display windows of the stores are always very well lit and it's all a very important part of the overall display to attract customers to stop, look and hopefully be tempted in to spend their money.

When you look at other stands around you at your first craft show, you will notice that those crafters who know what they are doing - have lights!

When you are deciding on your lights, there are certain things to take into account. They need to be sturdy and easy to carry around. Take the weight into account as well, you will have to carry them from fair to fair and at times, you will have to carry them upstairs or the length of long marquees.

Look around at various shops for your lights. You don't need to go for special - and normally expensive - professional shop display lighting. Nowadays, you can find plenty of choice in home decor or office supply stores.

The style of lighting will depend on your overall display. If you have a large sturdy framework, you can clip lights to that. If your display is more open, you probably need freestanding lights.

The right lighting will really make your stand and your beautiful, hand knitted designs stand out. And remember, the first part of making a sale is getting a customer's attention in the first place.

You will also need to have extension cables in your equipment pack, as you will often have to connect to the power supply at a distance.

Many organisers will require that you have your electrical equipment tested. A PAT certificate (portable appliance testing) is required for each piece of equipment and lasts 12 months.

There are all sorts of other things, you can add to your stand to attract attention and what you choose will depend on your style. You could decide to display one of your main pieces on a bust at the centre of your stand, lit by spotlights so that it catches the attention of the customers as they pass – or hopefully, don't pass! Or you could use a digital photo frame to showcase some of your other designs. If you knit garments, try to have photos of them actually being worn. If you knit soft furnishings, have some photos of them in place on sofas or in bedrooms.

If you knit beautiful, delicate Christening Robes, ask your friends and family to supply some photos of Christenings that have featured your work – oohs and ahhs can work wonders for your sales!

## Exhibition Banners

However you design your table, the first task of your stand is to be noticed.

You may well be in hall with 50, 70 or over 100 other craft stalls, so you want people to notice yours. You want them to stop, look at your work and of course you want them to buy. But if you don't attract them in the first place none of that can happen.

The exhibition banner displayed behind your table is a great way of doing this. It's an advert that people can see from a distance. You can include pictures of your hand knitting on the banner so that they have an idea of what you have on offer before they risk coming too close!

Many of the copy and print centres and some of the big stationery stores now produce this kind of banner or stand for you from about £50. So if you're planning on doing a number of events this can be a very good investment.

Do think of the design carefully. If you use a banner this will be your largest visual advert, so you want to make sure that it is sending the message you want and that it is giving people the correct idea about your style.

Make sure that you use the same colour scheme in the design of your banner that you have chosen for your display, your cards and packaging – it's your corporate image, and is just as important to your fledgling business as their corporate image is to any of the large chain stores, airlines or banks. All of your advertising material should be telling the same story.

### The rest of your equipment bag

There are other things that you need to make sure you have with you when you set out to do a show.

A cash float. Yes, I know the plan is to take money, but you also need to have some with you in the first place.

Most people get their money from cash machines nowadays, so they will be presenting you with beautifully crisp £10 and £20 notes. You will need to have some change for them if you want to make a sale.

Make sure you have a good selection of £5 notes, £1 coins, silver and copper if you're going to set your prices at £4.99, £9.99, £14.99 etc.

You also want to keep your cash safe. So you will need a cash box to make it easy to sort out your coins, and a bag that you can keep attached to you to keep all the hundreds of £10 notes safe.

You'll need a calculator to add up all the sales, a note book to keep a record of them and also to take notes for special orders that you will be sending out, so of course you'll need a pen!

Depending on how you have decided to display your hand knitting, you might need a supply of price labels, some paper bags or gift bags and tissue paper for packaging.

If you're working on your own, you'll need to take some food and drink with you as you might not be able to leave your stall. Once you get used to the fairs you are doing, you will know if food is available easily or if you can ask your neighbour to watch things for you.

Some organisers don't allow you to eat at your stand – and I wouldn't recommend sitting down to a large meal at any event, but a sandwich and a bottle of water can keep you going through a long day.

# Packaging your product

Obviously, when a customer buys a beautiful piece of hand knitting from you it has to be packaged in some way. But what way?

### Creating an image

In the world of marketing, image is vital, as we have been discovering.

Some brands are actually identified by their packaging as much as by their actual product.

Think of the duck egg blue box tied with a white satin ribbon. Since they were designed in 1837, the Tiffany blue box can be as important as the piece of jewellery inside it when someone is deciding to make a purchase. The same is true of many brands, whether that is the famous German teddy bear, the couture house selling their lipsticks and handbags or the fashion houses selling their unique brand of knitwear.

Packaging isn't simply to protect the purchase. After all, you could just put the scarf that the client has purchased in a clear plastic bag. I've even seen some crafters wrap their work in old newspapers (not knitted designs I have to admit!) and while that might save some money it certainly doesn't create much of an impression.

A piece of luxury hand knitting is never an absolute necessity. It might keep you warm but basically it's a treat, a little personal luxury and it should feel that way. So it's very important to put some thought and investment into your packaging.

After all, it is all part of your product and you should price it into your cost in the same way as you do the yarns and the special trimmings you use in a piece.

Hand knitting is a strange product in some ways. The value isn't really down to the actual materials but the perceived value of the piece, which is all to do with the standard of your workmanship, the amount of work in the design, the way you present it, where it's sold and how it is packaged.

We will assume that, seeing as you are reading this book, the standard of your workmanship has already reached a level that customers will be happy with.

The amount of work in a design can be a little bit more difficult to value. Obviously a very intricate piece of work will require a higher price. But there are some big brands, who can charge big prices but actually produce very basic designs. Well made but very basic!

Most people are not very good at judging the actual value of unique hand created designs, so the way you present and package it will create a pricing level.

A pile of knitted scarves piled up and squashed together on your stand will give the image of homemade items sold at a church or school fete. The same scarves each sitting in their own space with some draped across display stands to show the detail in your work  and each with a tag giving details of the fibres used and care instructions, will appear much more valuable, especially if you have some lovely individual gift boxes for each piece.

So even though a box will cost you extra, it would be a good investment if you are selling in the kind of market place where you can pitch your hand knitting at that level.

There are many ways of packaging between these two styles and this is an important decision, as it will set the style and image of your stand, indeed of your collection and your business as a whole.

So what can you choose and what image does it create?

This will of course depend on what range you are creating.

A large hand knitted aran afghan will need different packaging to a lace scarf and you will have to choose the physical type of packaging to suit your designs. Bags, tissue paper, boxes, wrapped in tissue and placed in a gift bag or encased in tissue, placed in a box and then put in a bag.

A luxury gift bag with cord handles will give an image of luxury. A brown craft bag will work with traditional or recycled design work. Bright coloured packaging is good for trendy designs and of course you can package baby designs into the baby gift bags you can find at a stationary supplier

## Packaging the packaging

Your packaging and presentation doesn't stop with physically protecting and wrapping the piece of work.

Think about how you are going to hand it over. After all, you not just going to hand somebody a cushion, you will want to put it in a bag, possibly a gift bag as we've just discussed, but there's more to it than that.

You must always include some form of business card. It could be a simple business card with your name or business name, your logo and contact details. Or it could be a special romance card giving some information about you, how you create your designs, what your inspiration is, or details about the specific piece of hand knitting and fibres you have used.

Look at the websites of some of the designers who work in your field, whether that is fashion, accessories, home design or toys. Read their descriptions and the home page of their site that gives the background story of the designer or the company.

Obviously you don't want to copy their wording, that would be copyright theft as well as very unimaginative! But there's nothing wrong in learning from the experts and gaining inspiration for your own business.

I had a friend at craft shows who put all her items in little boxes. The boxes were very nice, but the finishing touch was the fact that she tied them all with beautiful ribbon. It took a little bit of extra time, and it made every customer feel that she was putting a little bit of extra effort into their purchase. People didn't mind waiting, they didn't even mind waiting while she finished packing someone else's order. She had lots of repeat customers!

And of course the packaging can be an advert in itself. If you put your hand knitting into a lovely gift bag, which just so happens to have your logo hanging on a tag from the bag handle, then every one of your customers will be advertising you as they walk around the rest of the event. Just another little marketing idea you can liberate from the large stores and designer companies!

Choose your packaging to suit your image. There's a huge range of packaging available. You might choose natural jute or hemp bags to suit your hand knitting if you work with the natural fibres in chunky designs.

If you use fine fibres to create beautiful designs for babies, then you could use pale pink and blues and other pastel colours in your packaging.

Glamorous hand knitted garments might call for elegant black and gold bags, while delicate silk stoles might look perfect in silver hologram gift bags.

You could even buy plain craft bags and design

the whole look yourself, even having a rubberstamp made of your logo and printing the bags yourself.

# Pricing your hand knitting

Pricing your hand knitting can be one of the most difficult parts of setting up your own business.

Most people undervalue themselves and feel nervous at first about the idea of asking people to pay for the work they have created. But after all, if you are reading this book you have taken the decision to sell your handmade designs, and therefore you should expect to be paid for it. It is no longer a hobby and you shouldn't treat it as one. This is now a business

As I mentioned earlier in the book, hand knitting can be an odd product to price. It is more than the sum of its parts. In fact exactly the same yarns can be made into very similar pieces of hand knitting but priced a completely different levels depending upon where they are sold and how they are packaged.

It's one of those products, where your pricing is as much to do with what the market will stand as the actual costs of the materials.

Your reputation as a designer will also affect how much you can charge, so you will find that as time goes on you can price the same pieces at a higher level. Just ease the prices up gently as you do more shows.

And of course your presentation is a vital part of your pricing. As long as the quality of your work is good, if you present it as an exclusive piece then it will be viewed as more valuable.

## Work out the cost of each piece

One of the biggest problems people have when starting out selling their hand knitted designs is not to overprice it, but to underprice it.

They undervalue their work and potential customers see the price on the tag rather than what fibres, skill and time have gone into creating the pieces they are looking at.

And if you undervalue your own work, the potential customer will not see it as a wonderful opportunity to buy a piece of work at a great price, they will judge it as a cheap product even if you have used the finest yarns and trimmings.

Left to their own judgment, many people can only tell the difference between mass produced items from the Far East and unique hand created items by the price tag and the marketing.

So it's very important to pitch your self at the right level.

There are various stages to pricing your hand

knitting.

First of all, you obviously have to know the actual costs of your work.

Itemise each piece you have used in your design. How much yarn, how many beads or buttons, how much thread or elastic?

Also remember to include the cost of actually getting the stock, for instance the cost of the journey to the warehouse or wool shop or the delivery charge for the package if you're buying your yarns by mail-order or through the Internet.

Divide the delivery cost by the amount of balls of wool, skeins of silk or number of buttons you have purchased and add that amount to the price of each item.

For instance, if the delivery is £5.00 and you have bought 10 skeins at £10.00 each, then each strand actually cost you £10.50.

Another thing to remember is to add the VAT or other local taxes onto your individual price.

It can be far too easy to forget these extras when you're first working out your costs. When you place an order for a number of items, you're perfectly well aware of the total amount you have spent, but when it comes to working out the price of each individual skein, ball or button, it can be far too easy to look at the price label on the skein and forget everything else.

So when you start, take the time to work out these costs for each individual design you make.

Work out how much actual yarn you have used for each design and work out how much it cost you. Over a number of items the difference between three and three and a half skeins will really begin to add up.

Also take into account how much you have paid for buttons, beads or other accessories such as bag handles.

Once you have an accurate price for the components of your design you also need to take into account how long it took to make it, how much the packaging is going to cost, and how much it is going to cost you to sell it. For instance the commission you pay or how much rent you will pay for your stall must be added to your items. After all you have to pay it.

Another mistake that many new crafters make is to fail to take into account the cost of their labour, especially when they are expanding a hobby. Knitting takes time and if you are making complex items it can be a lot of time. Make sure that you include the cost of your time in your prices.

While there's no doubt that it is definitely a joy to be paid to do what you love doing, the important part there is 'to be paid'.

It might be all right to do your first couple of fairs for the love of it, but you must remember that you are investing your time in creating your hand knitted designs, sourcing the right yarns and trimmings, finding packaging and display material and the time you actually spend at the fair, and that time could be invested elsewhere. So you must include the labour costs in your calculation.

Time yourself when you are making one of your designs. Don't time the first piece that you make in that design because you will get faster once you've learnt a technique. Once you know how much time that design takes on average, you can decide how much you want to be paid for that time.

The final part of the equation is profit.

Profit isn't a dirty word. Every business, no matter how large or small needs to make a profit if it is to have a future. Even a charity has to make its own form of profit otherwise, after all the costs are paid it has nothing to give to the charity.

The level of profit that you want is entirely up to you, but don't set it too low.

### Your wholesale price

Once you've been through all the stages, and you've come up with the cost of producing each of your designs, you have the price that you must sell it at to avoid losing money. You could call this your wholesale price, the lowest price at which you can sell your hand knitting

It is a vital price to have even if you have no intention of wholesaling, although you may want to consider it if approached by a craft shop or gallery. But there will be times when you want to offer a discount on your prices, even if it isn't for wholesale.

You might want to give a discount to regular customers. You will need to give a discount to party organisers if you do party plan. You might want to run a promotion involving a discount or many other types of offer.

Your general price must be set so that it allows you to discount, and you can't discount below your cost price – there's no point in losing money on each sale you make!

So decide what your absolute minimum price is and then you will know how much you can afford to sell it for.

## Setting the price of your product

Now you know how much it actually costs you to produce a each of your designs, but that's only the first stage of deciding what you will actually sell them for.

As I said, don't be tempted to simply cover your costs and add a little bit of profit. If your hand knitted work is priced too cheaply it will be considered cheap.

At this stage you have to decide where you want to pitch your product. Who do you want to sell it to? Who do you have the opportunity of selling it to? At one end of the scale there is no point in selling your high quality unique designer pieces too cheaply because your potential customer will not see the value, they'll just see the price and you'll damage the number of sales.

But at the other end of the scale, there are times when you will want your hand knitting to appear inexpensive, for instance if you're selling small knitted hats for children at a school fair or inexpensive pot holders as pocket money gifts.

Although the biggest danger for new crafters in general, is to underprice their product, you also want to avoid overpricing it.

I also find that it's a good idea to have plenty of choice under £10 level. In fact at some fairs, under the £5 level. Although I will have exclusive pieces set in the £100 plus range, and it's very nice when they sell, the main turnover comes from impulse buys. Unless you're selling at very exclusive fairs, it's unusual to sell many individual items are over £100. That is the kind of fair and the kind of level you want to work up to, rather than the point that you start your career at.

In general, hand knitting is one of those products when the pricing comes down to what the market will stand. It can sound very imprecise and really quite unfair, but it is the fact.

Someone who has developed a name as a designer and is selling through a store or website or at a craft event that backs up the image of expensive designer pieces, can demand a much higher price for their hand knitted designer garments, even fairly basic designs.

If you look at some of the designer websites and in the department stores you will find quite basic garments that are very simply made of ordinary yarns selling for very high price tags, but that is partly because they have created a 'name' and customers are willing to buy into the image. It's something to aspire to rather than to start your career with.

The exact price that you decide on is up to you. Look around at your competitors to get an idea of the prices in your market area, but don't be tempted to simply undercut the lowest price.

In any market, selling anything, you will always find somebody who is willing to charge less. Their entire marketing plan centres around being cheaper than anyone else, but unless you can produce millions of items in China, and you can afford to lose enough money to undercut your competitors until they go bankrupt, there is absolutely no future in this business model.

No matter how low you set your prices, somebody will come along and undercut you.

Remember, it is perfectly possible to turn over millions of pounds and lose money, look at the banks! Profit is what will pay the bills when they come in and will allow you to invest in new yarns and buttons and book more fairs and events.

So do get a feel for the prices that others are charging for hand knitting that is similar to yours. Compare that to how much your costs are and find a price that you are comfortable with.

One of the great things about selling direct to your customer is that you can change your prices quickly if you feel it is necessary although you don't want to do this too often. For instance, you don't want to make a habit of selling a cushion cover at £20 one week and then £10 the next week, because you will upset your regular customers. But you can alter your prices up or down, and adjust them to the way the item is selling.

You could find that delicate lace shrug that takes a lot of making, sells out straight away every time and you can't keep up with that design.

Wonderful of course!

We all love the idea of selling out!

But you might still be able to sell as many as you can make if you put the price up. After all, if it doesn't work, you can always reduce it again or even put it on special offer!

# How to Promote yourself

Promoting your new hand knitting business can take a number of different forms.

The Oxford English dictionary defines 'promotion' as *an activity that supports or encourages a venture and the publicising of a product or venture, so as to increase sales or public awareness.*

Many people think of a promotion as being simply discounting prices, and while that is a valid method of attracting more customers, promoting your business can and should take many more forms than simply relying on price.

### Price promotions

We are surrounded by promotions in the retail world.

BOGOF's

50% discount.

Three-for-two

even 70% off!

January sale.

Christmas event

They can all sound very tempting, and some of them even work, attracting us to buy things we didn't really want and certainly didn't intend to buy.

But we have become quite jaded as consumers, simply not believing most of these promises. The half price sale finishes on Sunday and 50% off sale starts on Monday!

But that doesn't mean that you should completely forget about developing your own promotions and special offers, you just have to be a bit more imaginative with them.

### Bundled discounts

This is the type of marketing policy that covers things like the BOGOF that you find at supermarkets, but it doesn't have to be that obvious. Clearly, if you're going to offer Buy One Get One Free, the price of each one has to cover the costs of two.

You might decide that your marketing policy is to offer bargains, to be the discount outlet of the craft fair, in which case you've probably gone for bright, primary colours in your design and basic packaging as well as designs that you can produce quickly and easily – scarves created with thick yarn on big needles for instance. If this is your brand style you will want to make a show of your discount offers because this will be your main selling point.

But if your style is intricate hand knitting and

pieces in luxurious fibres, you don't really want your elegant craft stall to look like a supermarket. In this case you can still introduce the idea of bundled discounts in a more subtle way.

For instance, if you sell cushion covers and afgans that work together as sets, but you normally sell them separately, you can have a discount for buying the collection.

If you sell accessories for the kitchen you could have an offer where a customer who purchases four items, receives a fifth one free.

If you sell baby jumpers, jacket and hats separately you could have a discount price for the hat when it is purchased with a cardigan.

## Time specific discounts.

You could have a 'special show price' on a particular type of item. You can set a discount 'just for this event.'

You see this kind of promotion quite regularly at large events, Normally it's the kind of offer advertised by the large, professional companies that travel the country selling at flower shows, county shows, horse shows and the like. If you buy from them on the day, you pay a special show price. If you purchase later from their website, the item will cost you more.

The whole idea of this is to make people part with their money straight away, rather than picking up a leaflet, going away and thinking about it. It's a style of promotion that is quite often used for more expensive products, where people are more likely to go away and think about it rather than making an impulse purchase, but it can work on any type of product. The idea is to make people buy it now.

## Free gifts

Everyone loves something free.

Free is a magic word in marketing.

Free will stop almost anyone in their tracks and make them look.

So how can you use this marketing idea in your business.

Some people literally give something away free, for instance, they have a bowl of boiled sweets on the counter with the idea that this will make people stop and take a sweet. Of course they will stop and take a sweet and some of them might even look at your hand knitting while doing it!

I prefer to make people work for their free gift or more to the point, buy something.

The best way of using the free gift marketing method is to encourage people to buy more. Spend over £40 and receive a free crochet brooch. Spend over £60 on knitted toys and receive a free knitted cupcake. Spend over £10 and receive a free gift box. The exact details, the exact levels of spend, and the free gift is entirely up to you. It will depend on your style, the type of designs you create and your product range. It will depend on the type of customer you're aiming at, and it will depend on your profit margins.

## Sale time

The problem with the word Sale is that it has been overused and has lost its power to attract. Some shops constantly have sales and people stop looking.

But it can still be worth using. If you have some stock that just isn't selling, it can be worth bundling them all together and putting the word sale on the collection.

I would try various other methods first - altering the prices, up as well as down. Sometimes an item that is not selling will suddenly become a bestseller when you put the price up!

A bargain basket can be a very good way of selling designs that you want to reduce in price. There's something about a bargain basket or box that just attracts people! They love rooting through looking for a bargain. Of course you have to make sure that your hand knitting is not just going to end up in a tangled dirty mess at the bottom of the basket. How you manage this problem will depend on the designs you use in the first place. If you already package your hand knitting, then it should be safe enough in a basket. But if you normally have your scarves, jumpers or knitted toys laid out on the counter you might want to put each of them in a plastic bag first.

## Product promotion.

Although price promotions are fine to use at one time or another, you should have promotions that are a continual part of your business plan.

In other words, you should promote your business.

These types of promotions are to encourage customer loyalty, to create the style of your brand, to remind potential customers about you and of course to increase sales.

Make sure that everyone who has a piece of your hand knitting knows that it is one of your designs.

Some events, especially charity events, ask you to provide a gift for their raffle. And of course you want to support the charity, but make sure that whoever wins your piece of hand knitting knows where it's from. There's nothing wrong with supporting your business as well as the charity.

When a customer buys a piece of your hand knitting, make sure that they have the details of where they can find you and how they can contact you so that they can make future purchases. When someone receives some of your hand knitting as a gift, make sure they know that you are the designer and how they can purchase more pieces.

Every piece of hand knitting that leaves your stall should be branded in some way. The way you add your logo will depend on the style of your work and the type of product that you produce but don't think that it has to be something expensively produced by a professional printer.

The beauty of your hand knitting is that it is individually handmade, so there's nothing wrong with the packaging being handmade as well. In fact it adds to your overall style.

If you make a chunky vintage style cushion covers, why not find some manila luggage tags and write your details by hand on them. If your hand knitting is very delicate in fine fibres, create a delicate leaflet to put in the bag or box with it and wrap it in lovely tissue paper so that the customer knows it's a luxury item.

## Talking about your hand knitting

One of the nice things about selling face-to-face is the fact that you actually get a chance to meet your customers. So make the most of it.

They could buy a piece of knitting anywhere. At some of the other stalls at the fair, at any department store, homeware store or even at the supermarket. But they want to buy the unique pieces of hand knitted design from you. So talk to them about it.

When you look around at many events, you will always find some designers who just sit behind their stall, often reading a book.

Put yourself in the position of the potential customer.

If you were thinking of buying something from that stall, you'd probably just walk past. Why should you show interest in their work if they can't show interest in you. You also have to remember that a lot of people would feel uncomfortable about disturbing someone who has obviously got something better to do than to talk to them.

So, stand behind or to the side of your stall.

Smile at people, engage with them, say hello. You don't have to pounce on every potential customer - that is counter-productive. But you should show them that you are aware that they are there and that you are willing to talk to them if they would like.

When you do open a conversation, talk about your work. What makes it different? What is your USP (unique selling point). After all, you now know what your style is, so you should also know why your hand knitting is different to anyone else's.

Do you always work with ethically sourced fibres that are spun by hand?

Are your designs made from natural cotton?

Have your hand knitted soft toys been checked for all the safety regulations – in the UK home toymakers can follow a process to self-certify handmade toys to gain the required CE marking o meet the legal requirements of the Toy Safety Directive 2011.

You can also talk about what led you into designing and creating your work, what is your story?

Tell them that you can customise pieces, creating designs in different sizes or specific colours. Taking orders for bespoke hand knitting can be a very valuable addition to your new business.

And don't be afraid to talk to someone, even though you have a very good feeling that they are not going to buy anything from you, at least today. They may well come back on another day when they do want to buy some of your work, and they will remember that you were friendly and didn't pressurise them. Or you might sell to the people who were listening to your conversation - lots of people prefer to join a crowd when they wouldn't approach you themselves.

## Demonstrating your craft.

This might sound a bit odd, showing other people how to compete with you! But in fact, showing people how to do a craft can be a very good way of selling to them.

It can work in two different ways. You can create starter packs, so that you can teach people how to create their own hand knitted pieces. Next time you're at a large craft shop, look around at how many products are being sold to crafters. There's nothing to stop you put in your own product range together and selling these starter packs and creating your own patterns to sell to your students.

You should also have some of your own handmade designs with you when you demonstrate.

People who are interested in learning how to knit are interested in hand knitted designs. And while they will enjoy making their own, they are beginners, and your designs will be much more professional.

So don't be surprised when you sell some of the samples you've taken with you. In fact, that should be part of your plan! Also make sure that you take plenty of promotional literature.

You want them to be able to find you when they decide they want to buy a unique piece of designer hand knitting

You can do these demonstrations to a number of different groups. Some libraries have regular events for people to learn new skills. You might find that you can work with the girl guides or brownies or as entertainment at birthday parties. You could offer your skills to women's groups or maybe even set up a package and offer it for hen parties. Learn to think outside the box.

## Seasonal promotions

There are certain times of the year that are just made for hand knitting and especially hand knitted gifts.

The main ones of course, are Christmas and Easter and don't forget Mother's Day, and Father's Day if you create designs for men.

There are also some other dates that you might want to add to your list. Halloween is getting more and more popular, and there are plenty of people who love to dress up for Halloween and would certainly buy something unique if you offered it, how about some spooky black shawls finished with feather trim! Depending on your style, you can really go to town on some over the top Halloween designs – knitted pumpkins, spooky ghosts, even costumes for babies.

You might also be able to create designs as Valentine gifts and for first Communions and confirmations. If your design style lends itself to delicate boleros or beautiful bookmarks these celebrations would be perfect for you.

Which of these events you decide to use for your promotions will depend on the type of work that you design, and how and where you sell it.

You will probably be able to think of some more events that would be perfect for your new brand.

### The Christmas season

The Christmas season is arguably the most important part of the year for your new design business.

It's that time of the year when you will find the most events, and some of the biggest events.

The season runs from early October to about the middle of December.

The main out-of-town Christmas fairs are completed by the end of November or the very beginning of December and then events such as Christmas markets will run almost up to the holiday itself.

Some crafters spend most of the year preparing for the Christmas season, and for any crafter it can be the most hectic time of the year - in fact, it's best if you get your own Christmas family preparations done before October!

As a knitware designer this is an ideal season. Knitted items such an easy gift to give and it can cover the whole range of gift giving. The hat and scarf set is a standby for many gifts, but you can add all sorts of item to the list depending on what your product range is. Small accessories for the kitchen, a case for the new gadget, even the Christmas stocking that they will be packed in.

Your customers can find the perfect gift for almost anybody and it will be unique. Whoever they give it to won't be able to go to the January sales and see how much they spent! And they don't have to worry about someone else giving exactly the same gift - a problem you do have to consider when you choose a book or DVD!

All styles of hand knitting can be adapted for the Christmas gift market.

If you focus on fashion knitting and fun and funky designs then Christmas tree bauble hats and bright red and green jumpers or hats might be the way you decide to go.

On the other hand, you may prefer to simply make more of your normal designs and package them beautifully so that they are a gift that somebody can simply purchase and give, already boxed and ready to be presented, especially if you add a gift bag or gift wrapping.

The seasonal promotion doesn't just have to stop with your actually hand knitting and how you package it.

You can – and should - carry the idea through to your entire shopfront.

Again, take a leaf out of all the experts book. The department stores spend thousands of pounds decorating their windows. The shopping centres make a big feature of their Christmas decorations, and town centres make an entire event out of turning on the Christmas lights.

They invest in all this because it attracts customers, and it puts them in the Christmas mood, which makes them think of buying presents and spending money.

So join in. Decorate your stand. Use tinsel or fairy lights along the front. Maybe you have enough room for a miniature Christmas tree or your product range allows you to create unique knitted Christmas tree decorations or Christmas stockings.

Whatever you decide, make your stall festive, encourage people to think of buying Christmas gifts when they see your display.

If you have decided to use beautiful gift boxes as part of your promotion, display them on your table.

Think how the stores display all the beautiful gift wrapped boxes that they have on offer at this time of the year. Very often the products inside them are nothing special. Body lotions, shower gels, hand creams, maybe a china mug with some sweets inside it, maybe a tie and some cufflinks.

Many of these beautifully presented gifts contain quite ordinary products, but they are packaged in a beautiful way in beautiful boxes with ribbon around them. It's easy to just buy them, take them home and put them under the tree.

People are always short of time, especially at Christmas time, and buying this type of ready to give gift is so much easier to do.

It takes the thinking and the work out of the process. And at this time of the year, customers are attracted to anything that will save them time and make life easy. Yes, it would be cheaper to buy a nice box and all the body lotions and package them yourself, but people don't do that, they pay extra to have it done.

So when they see your hand knitting, beautifully packaged and presented it will automatically look more like a gift. And that's the effect you want.

This might also be a time to use one of the price promotions, again very often used by stores.

The most popular one is 3 for 2 - of course remember that it's always the lowest priced item that is free and to work out your prices to cover the cost of three!

This is another time you should learn from the experts. They have found that, particularly at Christmas, this promotion will encourage people to buy two items, rather than just one. In fact, you can find yourself spending longer in front of the shelves wondering who you will give the extra two gifts to and what you should choose, when it would be much quicker and cheaper to just pick the one you wanted in the first place. But that's the point. It works. So if the big stores can make the most of it - so can you.

Of course, do remember that they are all priced to cover the cost of the three items, even though as a shopper you feel that you are getting a bargain, and there's that wonderful magic word again –

FREE!

So if you decide to use this promotion, do make sure that you work out your prices correctly. You're not actually in the business of giving away your work – even at Christmas!

When you're selling at the Christmas season it's all about getting the sales.

People want to buy gifts.

They will part with their money.

They have to go home with all the presents they need.

The stocking fillers.

Small gifts for friends and neighbours.

The gifts for teachers.

They will spend their money somewhere, and your main aim at this time of the year is to get them to spend it with you. That is why you invest money in taking a stand at the fair in the first place.

Selling is the whole point of starting your business in the first place.

# Recording your progress

So far we have been looking at the actual process of selling.

Designing your craft, pricing it, finding fairs, how to set up your stall and display and sell your designs, how to make the most of seasonal events and where else to look for outlets for your business.

But you also have to remember that you are running a business and you have to learn to be businesslike in how you go about your work.

One of the most important parts of any business is learning how to be methodical and accurate in how you record everything about your business and keeping everything on the right side of the law.

## Keeping Score

It's very important to know exactly how your business is progressing. Keeping records might seem boring and unnecessary and most people prefer to avoid the paperwork, but it's vital.

First of all you need to keep accurate records of your stock.

Before you go into a fair make an accurate list of the stock you are taking and re-check it at the end of the day. *Do this every time.* It may seem like an unnecessary burden but it is the only way you will be able to accurately tell how your business is doing.

The detail you will go into depends on your product, but it needs to give you enough information to enable you to make judgements of what items are selling, which are most profitable and which you should concentrate on for the future.

Over a number of fairs you may also be able to see some pattern emerging, which means that you can tailor your stock to a specific market - type of fair, geographical area, time of year. You might find that the type of design or price range that you sell in one type of venue is dramatically different from another type of venue. It's tempting to think that you'll be able to remember, or you'll get a 'feel' for the type of stock you should take, but you'll be wrong. Once you actually look at the figures it can be quite a surprise to see what actually are your best sellers.

Keeping accurate records of each fair will also enable you to judge what effect a change of price has on your overall performance.

An increase in price may lower your actual sales but increase your profit. Then again, a lowering of your price may increase sales to such an extent that it also increases your profit. And of course there's always the confusing situation where an increase in price leads to an increase in sales.

You can only tell what will happen by trial and error and keeping accurate records so that you can actually plot what is happening from event to event. And selling at craft fairs is the ideal format for making such experiments.

It's much easier to make changes in your prices as you work through different events and places rather than in a shop with the same customers each week. But you can only learn and profit from these valuable lessons if you keep accurate records.

## The Business of Business

This book is mainly about marketing and selling your handmade craft, it is not intended to be a detailed guide to the legal, financial and tax requirements of running a business – any business of any size.

## Find some expert advice

There are many books and courses and websites available where you can find out about these other areas of running your business and I recommend that you invest some time and money in this information so that you can avoid any pitfalls and problems in the future. But the following pages are designed to be an introduction to the areas you will have to consider.

## Legal Requirements

First of all – records. You are of course in business, no matter how small your business is to start with.

Exactly how you choose to set up your business depends on your own circumstances and the size of company you intend to aim for.

There are many sources of information on setting up business - hundreds of books, packages from banks, guides from Local Enterprise Boards and leaflets from the Tax Office.

Study as many of them as you can, so that you understand what will be required of you.

## Forms of Business Organisation

In the UK, the law permits a range of business organisation types, from the sole trader or one man (or woman) unincorporated business at one end of the spectrum, to the massive public limited company at the other. Basically, there are three forms of business organisation available to those setting up an operation:

Sole Trader
Partnership
Limited Company

### Sole Trader

A Sole Trader is literally what the name suggests.

One person setting up in business alone.

That person can set up in business without any

formalities. All profits are deemed to belong to that person and are taxed as such, and any losses and debts are also the personal responsibility of that one person.

"A Sole Trader is any one person trading with a view to making a profit"

A Sole Trader can use his or her own name for the business or choose a trading name.

**Advantages –**

There are no formalities for setting up the business, you can just set it up on day one.

All the profits you make over the year belong to you - so do all the losses!

You have sole control of the business – no one else is going to dictate what you can do.

You can also close down without any formalities if you want to.

**Disadvantages –**

You may be short of start up money.

You have to provide all the management expertise

You are personally responsible for all the debts

Partnership

A Partnership is a coming together of two or more people to carry on business with a view to profit. It is created by agreement and partnership articles may be drawn up. It grew from the law of contract and the principals of agency as developed by the courts. During the latter part of the nineteenth century, partnership law was codified by the enactment of the Partnership Act 1890.

The definition of partnership in the Act is:

"the relationship which subsists between persons carrying on a business in common with a view to profit."

The law states that not more than twenty people can be in partnership, except for professional partnerships. (Lawyers, accountants etc)

You would be setting up a partnership if you decide to go into business with a friend or member of your family rather than they just working for your business..

**Advantages –**

You can raise more capital

The pressures of running a business are shared

The legal requirements for forming a partnership are very few. The 1890 Act just regulates what happens if partners have not agreed.

Profits and losses are shared.

**Disadvantages –**

You don't have sole control of the business

You are jointly and separately responsible for the debts (this can be a significant disadvantage if someone disappears!)

There can be problems if the partners disagree and cannot work their way through the differences.

## Limited Company

In English Law, a Limited Company is a separate entity artificially created. It can sue, be sued, be prosecuted and fined.

It is separate to the shareholders and the Shareholders liability is limited to their shareholding (the amount invested)

A Limited Liability Company can be defined as a legal person, separate from the owners.

If you are at the beginning of a craft business that you plan to grow and that requires larger amounts of capital investment in equipment and premises, such as a ceramics or glass company or creating homemade food or preserves, you may want to consider setting up as a limited company from the start.

**Advantages –**

Limited liability to the amount of the shareholding – so your potential losses are limited, although in practice you will normally have to sign personal guarantees if you want to obtain a large loan from the bank.

In theory it is easier to raise large sums of capital.

Companies can be professionally managed by directors.

Shares can be sold – even floated on the stock exchange if your company is large enough.

**Disadvantages –**

A Limited company is expensive to start (lawyers and accountants have to form it)

You have to file official accounts, which will normally involve working with accountants.

In the USA there are similar structures, the Sole Proprietorship, Partnerships, the LLC (Limited

Liability Company) and the Corporation. You should check your local business requirements and take the relevant professional advice.

## What does this mean for you?

Most craft businesses that will be trading at craft fairs in the UK or USA will be either a `sole trader' or a `partnership'. Either type of firm can employ other people.

If you intend to work on your own, or to employ others but to be `the boss' you will be operating as a sole trader - supplying all of the capital, earning all of the profits and being responsible for any losses. This is the easiest way to set up.

However, if you are setting up business with a friend or relative and sharing the financial input, financial responsibility and the decision making, you will be setting up a `partnership'. You will share the costs and the profits or losses. At this stage, no matter how good your friendship, you should set out some form of partnership agreement. In fact, an agreement can help to separate your friendship from your business relationship and it can reduce disagreements if all matters such as work load, responsibilities and the amount of investment in time and money are all discussed at the very start rather than just left as `understandings'!

## The Tax Office

Once you become self employed or earn a second income you have to take responsibility for your tax position and your National Insurance. You will have to fill in a self-assessment tax form at the end of each financial year and file it on time to avoid statutory fines.

Your local tax office will give you all the information you need, and you can also find plenty of help online from official sites, but basically you must keep records of all your income and all your business expenses. That is whatever money comes in from customers and whatever money you spend in order to carry on the business.

In the USA you should contact the IRS and check their website.

Wherever you are setting up a business, the most important thing to remember is that you are in business – even just doing a few craft events a year is a small business and you will have to notify the relevant tax office, even if your income is below the tax threshold. It's much better to be upfront from the start, rather than to risk getting your taxes in a mess later.

So, keep receipts and details of all that you spend for your business and all the money you take when you make sales. The easiest way to keep the records is to file and record all the receipts or invoices you receive for money you spend and record all the money you take at each craft fair or that you earn from special contracts.

There are many books and websites on bookkeeping and accounting for small business – this isn't meant to be one of them!  But the basic rules are – record everything!

Marketing for Small Businesses

Profit is not the amount of money you come away with on the day, or the amount of money you take overall. Profit is the difference between how much you take from customers and how much it costs you to do that.

So, keep an accurate record of all the money you take in – whether that is in cash or cheque and credit card payments – record every sale. This is your income.

Also record everything you spend to run your business – you have to have proof of this, so keep all your receipts and invoices safety filed, you will need them for your accounts and your tax return. If you spend £20 on paper for making your cards, paint for your art or thread for your sewing projects and don't get a receipt – you have just thrown that £20 away – you can't set it against your profits.

You can claim costs that you have legitimately incurred for running your business. So you can list the parts you use to create your products - obviously.

But if you need a new pair of scissors for your work, or you need to have business cards printed, or you choose to have a mobile phone that you only use for business, or the travelling expenses to get to and from the fair and the rent you pay to the organiser for your stand. The packaging material that you use when you sell your product, the cloth and display stands that you bought and the cash box to put your takings in are all legitimate costs. So is a college or correspondence course that you

126

have done to help you run your business, storage boxes and shelving that you use just for your business, or accounting or design software – all of these items and more are legitimate expenses and can be listed in your accounts.

But while creativity is important in most of your business - don't get too creative in the accounting part of it. Buying some new designs while you're away does not mean that you can claim your holiday as a business trip!

## VAT

The other type of tax that is involved in business in the UK is VAT – or Value Added Tax.

All of us pay VAT on things we buy but you don't normally notice it because it's included in the price on the label. Once you start buying wholesale the prices in the catalogues, on the website or in the warehouse will be plus VAT (which is 20% at the time of writing) and this can add quite a lot to your final invoice if you don't take it into account at the time.

As a business you can register for VAT and once your turnover of taxable goods and services reaches £79,000 you have to register for VAT.

Once you are registered for VAT you have to charge VAT on your products and you can reclaim the VAT you have paid on goods and services for your business.

Some items are zero rated – such as books (not e-books) baby wear and children's clothes, cakes and biscuits (although there are some very strange exceptions. Chocolate chip cookies are zero rated, but chocolate covered biscuits are standard rate).

If you are selling items that fall into this range it can be worthwhile registering voluntarily for VAT because in selling zero-rated items and buying standard rated items you would be able to receive a refund from HMRC (HM Revenue and Customs). You will have to submit regular VAT returns and there are statutory fines for being late in submitting them, so even if you are able to receive regular refunds on the VAT you have spent as a business you do have to put some work in for it.

The HMRC website (www.hmrc.gov.uk) has very detailed information about VAT as well as lots of information about starting a business, keeping records, tax and national insurance. It's worth spending some time reading through it.

In America the IRS (www.irs.gov/Businesses) also provides a great deal of useful information for setting up a business.

## Other legal requirements

Once you are in business it is also your personal responsibility to comply with all legal requirements.

Each industry has different requirements and it is up to you to research the industry that you are entering because ignorance of the law is no defence if you do run into problems.

For instance if you are going to be making jams and chutneys it is vital that you comply with all the labelling requirements listing ingredients, best before dates, your name and address and a number of other legal requirements. You would also need to comply with the food safety legislation. All of this legislation applies to you just as much as it does to a huge factory and although you may well 'get away with it' – you shouldn't even try! You are producing a food stuff that others will be eating and for your own safety as well as everyone else's you need to comply with the regulations.

If you are making knitted toys for children you have to comply with toy safety regulations and if you are making jewellery you have to follow the legal regulations for hallmarking precious metals and the regulations on nickel content.

Every area of business has its own rules and regulations and the best time to find out what they are is at the very beginning rather than when you find you've fallen foul of the law. There is a wealth of information available online and many specialist wholesale companies will also include information about legal requirements on their website.

### Insurance

You might think that you have good insurance cover, but your car insurance and building and contents insurance are not normally designed for business and might specifically exclude business use – so do check. It will be far too late to find out once you have to make a claim. Your insurance company could refuse to pay out even if your claim has nothing to do with your business.

It's also important to protect yourself by

ensuring that you have the correct product and public liability insurance as well as general business insurance.

Organisers will insist that you have insurance cover before they accept your booking, but you should have insurance anyway for your own safety. If you are a member of the National Market Traders Federation, your membership includes insurance and there are some insurance brokers who specialise in cover for craft workers, a web search will bring up a current list of companies who offer specialist insurance.

You should also be able to arrange cover if you are a member of a craft guild or association and fellow crafters will be glad to share information with you if you ask them. We all had to start sometime.

Although you must have liability insurance to be able to make a booking at craft fairs, you might also want to think about other business cover to insure your stock and any loss you might incur if you are unable to work or lose your stock through some disaster. The level of insurance that you might choose will depend on how much you have invested in your business and how large a part it plays in your overall financial picture.

You will also need to alter your car insurance as you will now be using it for trade rather than just personal use.

You should also check your home insurance. Many insurers will allow you to cover your computers used for business purposes at home, but some will not cover your home if it is used for business, especially if you have customers visiting you at home – do check.

# Growing your business.

## Where will you go from here

The decisions you make about the way you want your business to go and how you want it to grow are entirely personal.

They will depend on you, your personal circumstances, what you want to put into your business and what you want to get out of it. There is no right or wrong.

I have been in business since the late 1970s (oh, that makes me feel old - I started very young!) And for many years I ran a business with lots of staff, dealing with big multinational companies, and lots of overseas interests, and I loved it.

But things changed when I was diagnosed with M.E. (chronic fatigue syndrome). I had to make some rather drastic changes in my life.

Now, I design and make healing crystal jewellery. I mentor small businesses, and give talks to start up groups. I write books on business and alternative therapies, and I run my small family business through craft fairs and events and online websites. I can work from home and set my own timetable, and I love this as well.

When you start your own business, the whole idea is to have more control over your life.

If you are starting your hand knitting business as you leave college or university, you will probably have great plans for creating a brand that you will be able to launch into the mainstream, and that is wonderful. People with great brands that grow from small seeds are the lifeblood of the economy. That is how the great brands start. After all, Marks and Spencer started as a market stall in Leeds and Starbucks started with a single small store in Seattle.

If this is your plan, the process of selling face-to-face to your customer will allow you to develop your style. You will be able to get feedback about your designs and find out what people really like about it. And this will help you when you want to expand your business.

But there is nothing wrong with keeping your business small and under your own control. There are thousands of people who are making a comfortable living by designing and making hand crafted designs that they sell face-to-face to their customers. They have a loyal following and a regular season of events that they do year after year and they have no desire to start employing people and having their own business premises.

And you will find designer/ makers that fall into

the middle. They do have their own premises, maybe a workshop or a retail outlet and a small staff that help them run the business.

There are no rules, you just need to find a way that suits you and your lifestyle.

## Selling online.

Having a presence online can complement selling face-to-face.

When you are talking to people at a craft event you can direct them to your website or some of your other designs on etsy, folksy or Amazon or some other specialist site, depending on your product range.

You can use your blog to keep in contact with your regular customers, or create an e-mail list so that you can keep your customers up to date and let them know about the latest craft events.

If you do party plan you can have a website that you can direct potential customers to, where they can either see your range of hand knitting or they can make bookings for a party. You could even add a shop so that they can actually purchase from you on-line.

Social media is a wonderful way of keeping in contact with your customers and promoting your business. It gives the small business a voice, that kind of worldwide presence that was never imaginable just a few years ago.

The type of online presence that you choose will again depend on the style of your business, the type of hand knitting that you create and who your target customer is.

If your style is fun and funky hand knitting, then social media is probably perfect for you. If you specialise in beautiful silk and beaded wedding shrugs, your target customers will be mainly young women, and again social media is a perfect way of connecting with them and keeping in contact.

### The future

Once you've developed your style and have learnt what your customer wants you should have created a healthy and successful business with your handmade designs which will allow you to spend your time doing what you love.

The future direction of your business is entirely up to you, but you should never sit back and think you know it all!

Keep developing your style, keep adapting to changing fashions or trends. Keep your range and image fresh and relevant, it's far too easy to get complacent and stagnate, wondering why people aren't buying from you in the same way anymore. You might need to find new venues with new customers, you might need to freshen your display or introduce new designs. You need to be able to stand back and see how other people see your work and your display.

And change is fun!

Part of the joy of creating your own designs is the chance to learn new skills, working with new fibres and accessories and producing new designs.

So I wish you many years of exciting designing.

# A final word

## The Business of Business

This book is all about marketing and selling your handmade hand knitting, it is not about the legal, financial and tax requirements of running a business – any business of any size.

## Find some expert advice

There are many books and courses and websites available where you can find out about these other areas of running your business and I recommend that you invest some time and money in this information so that you can avoid any pitfalls and problems in the future.